Landscapes of
SARDINIA

a countryside guide
Second edition

Andreas Stieglitz

SUNFLOWER BOOKS

For Reinhard Michel

Second edition © 2006
Sunflower Books™
PO Box 36160
London SW7 3WS, UK
www.sunflowerbooks.co.uk

Published in the USA by
Hunter Publishing Inc
130 Campus Drive
Edison, NJ 08818
www.hunterpublishing.com

ISBN 1-85691-301-5

Golfo di Orosei: coast near Cala Gonone

Important note to the reader

We have tried to ensure that the descriptions and maps in this book are error-free at press date. The book will be updated, where necessary, whenever future printings permit. It will be very helpful for us to receive your comments (sent in care of the publishers, please) for the updating of future printings.

We also rely on those who use this book — especially walkers — to take along a good supply of common sense when they explore. Conditions change fairly rapidly on Sardinia, and *storm damage or bulldozing may make a route unsafe at any time*. If the route is not as we outline it here, and your way ahead is not secure, return to the point of departure. *Never attempt to complete a tour or walk under hazardous conditions!* Please read carefully the notes on pages 53 to 56, as well as the introductory comments at the beginning of each tour and walk (regarding road conditions, equipment, grade, distances and time, etc). Explore *safely*, while at the same time respecting the beauty of the countryside.

Cover photograph: Tharros (Car tour 5)
Title page: Nuraghe Is Paras (Car tour 3)

Photographs by the author
Maps by Pat Underwood, based on the official Italian IGM maps 1:25,000
A CIP catalogue record for this book is available from the British Library.
Printed and bound in Great Britain by J H Haynes & Co Ltd

10 9 8 7 6 5 4 3 2 1

Contents

4   Landscapes of Sardinia

ARTICLES

Foreword

Sardinia, the second largest island in the Mediterranean, is a walker's paradise off the beaten track. Travellers are overwhelmed by its scenic diversity, ranging from rough and primeval landscapes to gentle, golden sand dunes, from scorching rocky plateaus and windswept plains reminiscent of Africa to rolling hills with lush pastures and dense brushwood, from towering mountains cloaked in fine oak woods to a turquoise sea that touches the rocky coast. The fragrant Mediterranean *macchia* permeates the scenery, with colourful rock roses and an extravaganza of wild flowers flourishing in spring.

Enclosing fields and pastures, a myriad of stone walls patterns the landscape. Animal husbandry is still of great economic importance, and there is a lovely pastoral feel to the Sardinian countryside. Flocks of sheep graze on verdant grassy slopes, moufflons and wild boar roam the wild and rugged highlands, and eagles hover silently above. Steeped in history, Sardinia boasts thousands of *nuraghi* standing proudly in the countryside, ancient stone towers testifying to the famous Nuragic civilisation. Yet another asset is the excellent cuisine, a tasty combination of refined Italian and hearty Sardinian culinary skills.

Both occasional walkers and ardent trekkers are delighted by the unexpected and spectacular walking opportunities on Sardinia. The roof of the island culminates in the Gennargentu massif with the adjacent Barbagia — very rewarding walking territory which takes in the Punta La Marmora, at 1834m/6015ft the highest elevation on the island. The wild limestone massif of the Supramonte extends further east, with its glaring-white cliffs, densely-wooded slopes, steep-sided ravines and craggy defiles.

Only a stone's throw away from the lively Costa Smeralda, the serrated granite ridges of the Gallura in the northeast attract walkers for their remoteness. The massive upheaval of Monte Limbara rises near Tempio, its weird rock formations sculpted over millennia by wind and weather.

Separated by the Cixerri rift valley, the southwest comprises two great mountain ranges cloaked in dense oak woods, the Iglesiente and Sulcis. Occasional spoil heaps, abandoned miners' villages and old mine galleries bear witness to the past, when this region was extensively mined. Today it is a landscape of great scenic splendour, with good trails snaking through the hills and stunning vistas from the mountaintops.

The basalt plateau of Giara di Gesturi, a windswept plain rising in the fertile Marmilla region, is famous for its semi-wild horses roaming the sparse cork oak woods. Countless paths criss-cross this uniform tableland, where stone walls and some marshes provide the only landmarks.

Getting out into the countryside, you quickly leave all traces of tourism behind. Taste the real flavour of the island as you follow the walks and car tours described in this book. You will be richly rewarded for any effort. *Landscapes of Sardinia* puts this miniature continent in your pocket.

Benvenuti in Sardegna!

A word of thanks

I would like to thank all my friends who accompanied me on many walks with infinite patience. They made this task even more wonderful. I am especially grateful to my mentor Reinhard Michel, a lover of the island whom I would like to thank for his company on many trips to Sardinia. Once again, I would like to thank the publisher, Pat Underwood, for her unflagging enthusiasm, which has made this book possible. Last but not least a very special thank you to all those lovely people I met on Sardinia, locals and travellers alike. *Tante grazie a tutti!*

Recommended books

Landscapes of Sardinia is a practical touring guide to countryside exploration which should be used in conjunction with standard guides. General guidebooks for Sardinia include those published by Dorling Kindersley (Eyewitness Guide), Insight Guides, Rough Guides and Lonely Planet.

Literature

Sea and Sardinia by D H Lawrence

Novels and short stories by Grazia Deledda, the Sardinian Nobel Prize winner

Padre Padrone by Gavino Ledda. The autobiographical novel of a shepherd's son.

Introduction

How to get there

There are now many **flights** (including budget) from major UK airports direct to Sardinia. All year round you can fly to Cagliari (the capital) in the south (daily with easyJet from Luton or three times a week with BA from Gatwick), Olbia (near the Costa Smeralda) in the northeast (da ly with easyJet from Gatwick) or Alghero in the northwest (daily with Ryanair from Stansted). In high season there are also weekly flights from Gatwick, Southampton, Stansted, Heathrow, Manchester, Birmingham, East Midlands and Bristol. You will find the usual international as well as Sardinian car-hire firms at any of Sardinia's airports.

If you **take your own car and travel by ferry**, you can sail from Nice, Savona or Livorno to Calvi or Bastia in northern Corsica (3-4 hours), then drive down to Bonifacio for the 50-minute sailing over to Santa Teresa di Gallura (sailings are bookable online at: www.corsicaferries.com).

Getting about on the island

A **car** is essential for most walks described in this book — and it is certainly the most convenient way of getting around the country. Fully comprehensive insurance is strongly recommended if you take a rental car. Generally you must pay a deposit, except for payments made with a credit card. Make sure that the car is in good condition, too, before taking it out on the roads; any damage should be recorded in the contract.

From a walker's point of view, **public transport** is rather limited. Major towns and cities are served quite well, but not the more remote countryside where you will want to walk. There are **trains** connecting the major cities, including several branches of the very scenic narrow-gauge railway which is a delightful experience. Even **buses** are rarely useful to the walker, since they stick to the main roads and don't pass near the starting points of most walks described here. However, they *do* connect even the most remote villages, if only once a day. Most buses (except for the urban lines) are operated by ARST and are painted blue. Where a walk *is* accessible by bus, I have mentioned this, but timetables must be checked by telephone or at the nearest bus kiosk. Tickets must also be purchased from a kiosk

Narrow-gauge railway at Nurri station

before boarding the bus! If you want to be picked up by a passing bus, you have to give a clear hand signal — even when waiting at a bus stop. To let the bus driver know that you want to get off at the next stop, just ring the bell. Note that bus stops are not always clearly marked.

Except for the major towns and airports, **taxis** are not easily found. They are hardly an alternative to hiring a car.

Where to stay

Sardinia offers a wide range of accommodation in all categories and prices, from self-catering apartments (usually rented out per week; you have to bring your own linen) to classy hotels. Most establishments are spread along the coast, sometimes clustered in small resorts or ports. There are also hotels in all the bigger towns — convenient if you depend on public transport. In recent years *agriturismo* has become quite popular. These are holidays on a farm, where guests generally sleep comfortably and eat well — at a very reasonable price. Details can be found in special magazines on sale at kiosks; the tourist offices are also helpful in finding a place. While it's necessary to book well in advance for July and August, this is rarely necessary in low season. Many hotels are closed out of season (October-April).

The small village of **Aritzo** is the ideal base if you want to hike in the central Gennargentu massif and offers a number of good hotels. **Cala Gonone** and **Santa Maria Navarrese**, two friendly ports facing the Gulf of Orosei, are ideal for those who prefer being near the sea while enjoying the wonderful mountainous backdrop of the Supramonte. **Tempio** is the main centre of the Gallura and a good base for exploring the northeast of the island. On the west coast,

Bosa with its lovely old town and nearby port is convenient for exploring Monte Ferru and the surrounding mountains. In the southwest, which comprises the Iglesiente and Sulcis regions, your best bet is to drive along the coast and just look for a place that appeals to you.

The **official hotel guide**, *Annuario Hotels & Campings*, published by the Sardinian Tourist Authority (ESIT) appears annually and lists all hotels and camp sites, with current prices. Contact them for a free copy: ESIT (Ente Sardo Industrie Turistiche), Via Mameli 97, 09124 Cagliari, Italia; tel (0039) 070 60231; fax (0039) 070 664636. There is also a free-phone number when you are calling from within Italy: 800-013153; e-mail: esiturismo@tiscalinet.it

Climate and time to travel
Sardinia is characterised by a typical Mediterranean climate, with very hot and dry summers. Spring and autumn are the ideal seasons for walking. The months of March to June are best for flowers, although you do have to reckon with changeable weather and occasional rainfall. September and October have more stable weather and pleasant sea temperatures for swimming. July and August are far too hot for walking. It can be rather cold and wet in the winter, with snow occasionally falling on ground above 1000m/3300ft. At any time of the year, a strong wind might blow up (called the *maestrale* if coming from the northwest).

Language
Italian, the official language, is spoken by everyone, but many people (especially among the older generation) also speak Sardinian. Excepting in the larger hotels, English is not widely spoken on Sardinia, so a few words of Italian will be helpful. Take a pocket-size phrase book with you.

Nuragic culture (1500-500 BC)
Sardinia flourished during the Bronze Age. Its pre-historic Nuragic culture was named after the cyclopean round towers *(nuraghi)* built from huge, rough-hewn stone blocks during this era. These people created the most advanced megalithic buildings within the Western Mediterranean region. It is estimated that there were up to 10,000 *nuraghi* at the height of this civilisation; more than 3000 are still extant today, in varying states of preservation.

Nearly all *nuraghi* were placed where they could be seen from far afield, and prominent enough to act as a deterrent to potential aggressors. A typical *nuraghe* comprised a round tower, which tapered slightly towards the top and had an inner space covered by a false vaulted ceiling (see title page photograph and the panel on page 36). This consisted of increasingly protruding rings of built-up stones forming a dome *(tholos).* The larger *nuraghi* had two or three floors. It was not uncommon that *nuraghi* were extended into complex fortifications over the centuries, by adding a turreted ringwall around the central tower. These masterly fortifications clearly indicate the military nature of Nuragic culture. Despite sharing a common language and culture, individual tribes also fought amongst themselves. In times of military conflict with neighbouring tribes, the *nuraghi* served as keeps as well as places of refuge. In peaceful times people lived in little villages of closely-arranged round huts, similar to the shepherds' hut shown on page 111 (left).

Nuragic culture did not flourish in splendid isolation, but in the context of constant economic and cultural exchange with other Mediterranean cultures. Sardinia was obviously a very valued trading partner, on account of its rich mineral resources (particularly its copper ore deposits, a relatively rare asset in the eastern Mediterranean). Thus the Nuragic culture benefited significantly from extensive contacts with Cyprus and the Mycenaean culture, and subsequently with the Phoenicians.

Around 1000 BC the Nuragic people started to produce elaborate bronze statuettes which were displayed at places of worship, but also widely exported. These depict people from all social layers, wild and domestic animals, demonic creatures, little ships and tools, and appliances of various kinds. Like a photo album, these statuettes convey very direct insights into the social order of the Nuragic people. They show tribal chiefs, warriors and priests, shepherds and farmers, musicians and craftsmen, people suffering diseases and those recovered from disease. Some of these precious *bronzetti* are displayed in the national museums at Cagliari and Sassari; two are illustrated on page 126.

A geological overview

Together with the neighbouring island of Corsica, Sardinia once formed a tip of the original European continent. During the Tertiary period this land mass became detached and gradually drifted into the Mediterranean. In contrast to the Italian mainland, which is relatively young in terms of the earth's history, the islands of Sardinia and Corsica emerged more than half a billion years ago — a considerable period of time even in geological terms.

Walking on the island is like taking a journey through the history of the earth.

Almost three-quarters of Sardinia's surface is covered by rock dating back to the Palaeozoic era. In the Carboniferous period particularly, molten rock penetrated the earth's crust, and the solidifying magma left behind a massive plutonic rock formation, consisting primarily of granite. This Sardinian-Corsican batholith today forms the base of the two islands. All older layers of stone were thrust upwards in the process, under the influence of heat and pressure, partly converted into crystalline slate and lifted above sea level. Wherever these layers of stone have been eroded in later eras, granite emerges, sometimes cropping out over wide areas. Granite landscapes are very common in the eastern part of Sardinia, for instance in the Gallura.

During the Mesozoic era Sardinia experienced a period of relative calm. During this time, the landmass subsided and rose slightly several times, which meant that large areas were repeatedly flooded by the sea. During one period of flooding which lasted several million years, sub-marine deposits accumulated on the flooded surface, forming a layer of limestone and dolomite sediments several hundred metres thick. These sediments, which were largely deposited during the Jurassic and the Cretaceous periods, were largely eroded after the sea retreated during the Tertiary era. Today only a few remains can be found, for instance in the Supramonte at the Gulf of Orosei and in the Nurra. It is in these limestone and dolomite areas that most of the famous Sardinian caves can be found.

Towards the end of the Cretaceous period a phase of global continental drift began, which reached its peak during the Tertiary era. Where the continental plates collided, enormous mountain ranges like the Alps were thrust up in 'folds'. In other places the tectonic deformation of the plates led to new land masses being formed or even the tearing apart of continents. Europe and Africa were separated from America, and the Atlantic Ocean began to form. The Sardinian-Corsican landmass was separated from the European plate, and moved from its original place in the Golfe du Lion to its present position.

During this process Sardinia was stretched and pulled. The island broke apart into several massifs, which later lifted or subsided. A gigantic rift began to emerge which runs through the entire island, from the Gulf of Cagliari in the south to the Gulf of Asinara in the north. In addition, strong volcanic activity occurred, as magma could rise to the surface along the many crevices and fissures in the earth's crust. Enormous quantities of thinly-flowing lava poured over the western half of the island. Leaving mainly trachyte and tuff behind, these massive layers of volcanic rock— sometimes up to 1000m/3300ft thick — crop out over wide areas, forming large plateaus. In a second, much less significant, volcanic phase, basaltic lava flooded the central part of western Sardinia. As a thin top layer of basalt, it covers mountain plateaus like the Altopiano di Abbasanta and the Altopiano della Campeda. In the Marmilla and the hinterland of the Gulf of Orosei, these volcanic structures from the Pliocene epoch appear in the form of small basaltic table mountains.

Flora

Evergreen sclerophylls (woody plants such as the holm oak, with leathery, water-retaining leaves) predominate on Sardinia at altitudes up to around 800m/2500ft. Where the soil is acid, particularly on granite, the holm oak (*Quercus ilex*) is replaced by the cork oak (*Quercus suber*) which is also an evergreen. Although cork oaks can grow to an imposing size and stature, they are rarely given the chance to develop to their full natural potential, as the bark is regularly peeled in order to harvest the cork. For this reason, light woodlands with small trees predominate, which are rich in undergrowth. Half-wild pigs are left to graze these forests for the nutritious acorns.

At higher altitudes (above 800m/2500ft), light deciduous woods with stands of downy oaks (*Quercus pubescens*) are common. The downy oak has a familiar appearance, similar to the oak trees common in Western Europe. A multitude of shrubs and herbs thrive in its undergrowth, including the peony (*Paeonia mascula*) and the endemic hellebore (*Helleborus lividus corsicus*) with its pale green flowers.

Cork oaks near Tempio

Lovely groves of sweet chestnut trees *(Castanea sativa)* can be found in certain places at the same level as the downy oak. Not originally native to Sardinia, the sweet chestnut now forms sizeable stands along the hillsides of the Gennargentu.

A mainly evergreen shrub woodland of up to 5m/15ft in height is referred to as *macchia* on Sardinia. It typically features species like tree heather *(Erica arborea)* and the strawberry tree *(Arbutus unedo)*, which thrive on acid soil. In autumn the strawberry tree carries groups of ruby fruit reminiscent of strawberries. These are edible, but not very tasty, which presumably led to their Latin name 'unedo' — 'one is enough'. Another very common shrub is the lentisk *(Pistacia lenticus)*. It is spared by grazing animals and by the sun because of the high tannin levels in its leaves which remain dark green even in the hottest summer sun. Other common plants of the *macchia* are *Phillyrea sp* which prefer limestone, the aromatic myrtle *(Myrtus communis)*, and wild olive trees *(Olea europaea var sylvestris)*. The round bushes of tree spurge *(Euphorbia dendroides)* are often found on limestone areas near the coast; they can reach up to 2m/6ft in height. The tree spurge carries brilliant yellow flower clusters in spring; during the dry season it quickly loses its leaves. Another remarkable plant growing to the same height is giant fennel *(Ferula communis)* with its yellow flower heads.

Rock roses contribute to the floral magic of the *macchia*. The white-flowering Montpellier rock rose *(Cistus monspeliensis)* prefers acid soil and is therefore particularly common in granite landscapes. Its strong scent contributes to the characteristic smell of the *macchia* and protects the plant and its sticky leaves from being eaten by animals. Another species spared by grazing animals is the asphodel *(Asphodelus sp)*, which belongs to the lily family. In the gravel beds of mountain torrents and along river banks, you will come upon stands of oleander bushes *(Nerium oleander)*. When their pink-red flowers open in the summer, they create a spectacular array of colour. However, care should be exercised: this evergreen shrub which can grow up to 4m/12ft in height is extremely poisonous.

Plants which were originally imported to Sardinia but meanwhile have become part of the island's flora include the prickly pear *(Opuntia ficus-indica)*. This yellow-flowering cactus which reaches up to 5m/15ft in height is grown for its juicy (but prickly!) fruit and as an impenetrable hedgerow fencing for grazing land.

# Picnicking

The varied landscapes of Sardinia provide good opportunities for picnics. Shady woodlands are sometimes the setting for organised picnic sites which have been laid out with tables, benches and fireplaces; some have washing facilities and toilets. All organised picnic places along the routes of the car tours are indicated on the touring map and in the touring notes by the symbol ⩎. Below is a small selection of particularly pleasant places you might enjoy; all are highlighted on the touring map by the symbol *P* printed in green. If the picnic is well off the beaten track, along the route of one of the walks, the 🚗 symbol on the relevant large-scale *walking* map shows the nearest parking place.

Remember to wear stout shoes if you have to walk any distance — and take a sunhat. All picnickers should read the country code on page 55 and go quietly in the countryside.

1 LAGHETTO SANTA DEGNA (touring map) ⩎
by 🚗: see Car tour 1 at the 124km-point; 2min on foot. The Laghetto Santa Degna, a pond surrounded by a small park with picnic tables and benches, lies in a hollow above the village of Aggius.

2 N S DI CASTRO (touring map; photograph opposite)
by 🚗: see Car tour 1 at the 167.5km-point; no walking. Enclosed by typical Sardinian pilgrims' shelters, the beautiful Romanesque pilgrimage church of N S di Castro is a peaceful haven. There are some stone benches along the perimeter wall, and a large tree provides shade.

3 CASTELLO DEI DORIA (touring map) ⩎
by 🚗: see Car tour 1 at the 202km-point; about 10min on foot. Dominated by the ruined Castello dei Doria, the village of Chiaramonti is strategically situated on a limestone hill affording a splendid panorama of the surroundings. A short stroll leads through the narrow alleys of the old town up to the ruined castle, from where you enjoy a splendid view in all directions. There are picnic tables and benches here, but *no shade.*

4 FORESTA PIETRIFICATA CARRUCANA NEAR MARTIS (touring map; photograph opposite) ⩎
by 🚗: see Car tour 1 at the 210.5km-point; no walking. At the Foresta Pietrificata Carrucana you will see the petrified trunks of juniper trees dating from the Tertiary period scattered on a grassy hillside. Down by the nearby river there is a small fenced-in picnic site with a few tables and benches, where you also find some shade.

5 MONTE TONNERI (map page 104; nearby photos pages 106, 107) ⩎
by 🚗: following Car tour 2, take the right turn after 149km, CASERMA MONTARBU 11 KM, then see Walk 15, page 105, for details of the 10.5km long access road to the state forest of Montarbu/Monte Tonneri; no walking.

PICNIC FOOD

You can buy everything you need for your picnic basket in the local shops or in a supermarket. Fresh fruit and vegetables are sold in shops called *frutta e verdura*. There are some very tasty cheeses on offer, including the famous sheep's milk cheese (*pecorino*), of which there are many different varieties, depending on whether it is still fresh and soft (*ricotta*) or more ripened and mature (such as *pecorino sardo*).

For bread there is a wide choice of different kinds of wheat bread and buns in all shapes, you get it in *panetterie* and super-markets. The most famous speciality, *pane* *karasàu* (*'karasàrau'* means 'become hard') originally came from the shepherd villages of the Barbagia. It is baked in wafer-thin round slices and kept as a dry bread for weeks. Shepherds used to take it with them when they grazed their animals in areas far away from the village. Warmed up with a few drops of olive oil and a little salt, *pane karasàu* is served in restaurants, a real treat with the first sip of wine. It is also very tasty as a first course, softened in stock and served with tomato sauce, ample sheep's milk cheese and a fried egg. Called *pane frattau*, this is served even in the better restaurants. Wine is produced locally and usually bottled in the municipal cooperative, called *cantina sociale*. The best-known wine is made from Cannonau grapes, which are mostly culti-vated in the mountains, especially the Barbagia. It is a fairly dry, full-bodied and slightly fruity red wine packed with ripe berries.

Good mineral water is bottled in many places, so you don't have to buy water imported from mainland Italy. Spring water is also excellent.

Photographs: the petrified forest near Martis (Picnic 4, left) and N S di Castro (Picnic 2, right)

Near the forestry station there are picnic tables and benches in the shady wood; fountain.

6 CHIESA SAN PIETRO DI GOLGO (map page 84) 🍴

by 🚗: from Baunei (Car tour 2 at the 232.5km-point), follow the access route to Walk 9 on page 83; no walking. Near the enclosed church of San Pietro there are picnic tables under gnarled old olive trees.

7 SU GOLOGONE (touring map) 🍴

by 🚗: drive to the large car park on the leafy banks of the river Cedrino (Car tour 2 at the 314.5km-point); 2min on foot. Behind and below the chapel of N S della Pieta, the spring of Su Gologone (the largest on Sardinia) rises from a deeply-etched, turquoise-glimmering cleft in the limestone rock. There are some picnic tables and benches on the shady river bank.

8 SANTA VITTORIA (touring map; photograph page 35)
by 🚗: from Serri continue to the car park at the Nuragic sanctuary of Santa Vittoria (Car tour 3 at the 86km-point); less than 5min on foot. From the visitor centre, follow the gravel track straight ahead for a few minutes, until it swings right. The chapel of Santa Vittoria stands just at the steep cliff-edge of the plateau; in front of it is the Nuragic holy well described in the panel on page 35. You can sit on a wall for your picnic.

9 GIARA DI GESTURI (map page 109; photograph page 111)
by 🚗: from Tuili (Car tour 3 at the 134km-point) follow the access to Walk 16 on page 108; about 5min on foot. From the car park follow the beginning of Walk 16 for a few minutes, to the Chiesetta Santa Maria, where you can rest on basalt rocks under shady trees.

10 GROTTA SU MANNU (map page 124) 🏕
by 🚗: following Car tour 4, take the left turn after the 232km-point that leads to the Grotta su Mannu. After 1.4km you reach the car park at the entrance to this fine limestone cavern; no walking. Picnic tables and benches under shady trees, fountain, bar. For more information on the cavern see Walk 20, page 122.

11 SANTA CATERINA DI PITTINURI (touring map) 🏕
by 🚗: follow Car tour 5 to the coastal resort of Santa Caterina di Pittinuri (57km); 2min on foot. Behind the beach there is a shady picnic area with tables and benches in a small valley.

12 MONTE FERRU (touring map) 🏕
by 🚗: see Car tour 5 at the 79km-point; no walking. This shady picnic area with tables and benches is just by the roadside; fountain.

13 SAN LEONARDO DE SIETE FUNTES (touring map) 🏕
by 🚗: see Car tour 5 at the 88.5km-point; 3min on foot. There is a shady park with tables and benches above the road, with seven springs (hence 'Siete Funtes') bubbling in its upper part. The surroundings are wild and romantic, although somewhat neglected. Lichen hangs from branches, ivy creeps up the gnarled old trees, and mossy rocks make this wood a fairy-tale setting. If you want to escape the heat of the coast, you will find a cool and shady haven up here.

14 CHIESA SAN MAURO (touring map)
by 🚗: see Car tour 5 at the 169.5km-point; 2min on foot. The country church of San Mauro is set in tranquil surroundings and enclosed by typical pilgrims' shelters (kumbessias). You can picnic under the big tree at the church or in front of the kumbessias. See panel on page 45.

15 SA PUNTIGHEDDA (touring map) 🏕
by 🚗: see Car tour 6 at the 162km-point; no walking. The shady picnic area of Sa Puntighedda, with tables and benches, is next to a forestry house. There is a fountain by the roadside.

16 MONTELEONE ROCCA DORIA (touring map)
by 🚗: see Car tour 6 at the 268.5km-point; no walking. There are several pleasant places for a picnic in this village — for instance, the small square in front of the late Romanesque parish church of San Stefano or a little bit further uphill at the small church of Sant'Antonio (benches).

✿ Touring

On Sardinia remote scenery can be enjoyed without even getting out of your car. Despite many new roads, most places have fortunately preserved their feeling of wilderness. The six suggested car tours (covering almost 1600km/1000mi) take in the most scenic parts of the island, giving you an overview of Sardinia's varied landscapes. Each tour is designed to take in the main attractions in that particular area and to provide as much variety as possible. The tours are arranged in such a way that they may be easily combined, allowing you to drive round the whole island. But, realistically, you will probably only be able to cover perhaps three of these tours in a single holiday, especially if you want to walk as well.

Most tours are too long to complete in one day if you drive at a leisurely speed to enjoy the scenery. Consider spending a night en route, rather than trying to rush back to your base. Driving is slow on the winding roads in the mountains. The touring notes are deliberately brief and concentrate on giving accurate driving instructions (*signposting to be followed* is highlighted in SMALL CAPITALS). Most of all I emphasise possibilities for **walking** and **picnicking** — all the walks and picnics in the book either lie on the main routes or are reached via short detours.

The **fold-out touring map** is designed to be held out opposite the touring notes and contains all the information you will need to follow the suggested tours. Due to its small scale, only major, secondary and relevant minor roads have been included (I recommend the 1:200,000 map published by the Touring Club Italiano for detailed information). Lack of space prevents us from printing all town plans, so I give you clear guidance through all built-up areas. The **symbols** used in the text correspond to those on the touring map and are explained on the touring map key. Distances quoted are *cumulative kilometres* from the starting point.

Most of the **roads** are in very good condition, with an asphalt surface. There are still some gravel roads *(strade bianche)* which are rather a strain if you follow them for long distances. Most country roads pass straight through villages, where you should *drive with extra caution:* reduce your speed and be prepared for the unexpected. Anywhere on Sardinia, livestock and dogs roam freely on country roads.

TOUR 1: GALLURA AND ANGLONA

Palau • Porto Cervo • San Pantaleo • Arzachena • Aggius • Tempio • Passo del Limbara • Chiaramonti • Martis • Bulzi • Castelsardo

247km/153mi; approximately 12 hours (two days)
En route: Picnics 1-4; Walks 1 and 2

Comprising the northeastern corner of Sardinia, the landscape of the Gallura is predominantly granite. It derives its name from *gallo* ('cock'), the heraldic beast of the Viscontis, a noble Pisan family who ruled over this region at the height of the Middle Ages. Countless bays and inlets, bizarre granite cliffs and rocky offshore islets rising from a sea shimmering in turquoise and azure — the natural splendour of the Gallurese coast is overwhelming. In the 1960s, Prince Karim Aga Khan and his consortium began to develop the Costa Smeralda ('Emerald Coast'), engaging internationally renowned architects such as Jacques Couëlle and building an exclusive holiday paradise for the jet set. Strict regulations and limited planning permissions helped to create a touristic world of classy hotels, apartments, marinas and golf courses along this splendid stretch of coastline extending north of Olbia for some 55 kilometres. But in contrast to the bustle and the smart set on the coast, the interior of the Gallura is a remote mountainous region where time seems to stand still. Totally different again is the Anglona to the west, with its market towns and Romanesque churches built by the Pisans. These rolling hills are characterised by volcanic trachytes and tuffs alternating with Tertiary sediments. The old ruined castle of Castelsardo rises like an eagles' nest on the coast.

Opposite **Palau** (⛰🛏✕🛒), a harbour from where the ferry sails to Maddalena (Walk 1), the Archipelago della Maddalena spreads out before you, and the straits of Bocche di Bonifacio separate Sardinia from Corsica. Turn sharp right at the road junction with traffic lights where you enter Palau (brown signpost: MOLO TURISTICO/ROCCIA DELL'ORSO). Follow the road straight ahead, ignoring a sharp right turn to Le Saline/Cannigione. When you meet a T-junction at **Capo d'Orso** (4km; snackbar), leave your car for a short climb up famous Bear Rock, described in the panel opposite.

Return from Capo d'Orso the way you came, until you can fork left for LE SALINE/CANNIGIONE. Follow this road straight ahead, then take the left turn signposted to CANNIGIONE. Soon you cross a sandy dam separating a bay and a *stagno* that extends inland (8km). The coastal road winds its way along the Golfo di Saline (🎋 15km). Pass through the

Ascent of Bear Rock

Allow 40min return and a climb of 60m/200ft
Turn left at the T-junction and follow the road to the gated entrance of an old military compound. Fork left by an information board in front of the iron gate on a path running through greenery, initially following a crumbling stone wall. The path climbs between rock outcrops, then continues as a stone-cobbled footpath that zigzags uphill. An old military lookout post stands on the rise. Here you turn right on a stone-cobbled footpath. After descending briefly, the path leads you over to Bear Rock. From below this rock overhang there is a magnificent view of the Archipelago della Maddalena off the north-eastern tip of the island (cover photograph). The largest islands are Maddalena and Caprera, while the mountains of Corsica rise in the hazy distance. Return to the military outlook and clamber over some rocks, to reach the viewpoint shown above, where the 'Bear' rises in front of you.

TAFONI

In the eastern half of Sardinia granite is very prominent. Its manifold fantastically-eroded forms add to the special attraction of landscapes like the Gallura. Weathering creates sandy-grained granite detritus and large rounded blocks of stone, which — due to their characteristic form — are referred to as 'wool sacks'. When erosion continues and more detritus is washed away, these 'woolsacks', which are initially below ground level, appear above the earth's surface. Sculptured over millennia by wind and weather, the granite rock is modelled as if by artist's hand. Bizarre hollow structures are created which, after the Corsican word for window (*tafone*) are called *tafoni*. Many *tafoni* together can create web-like structures, and sometimes the rocks are entirely riddled with *tafoni* holes. In Gallura these caves created by weathering are referred to as *konki* (*konki* meaning 'hollow'); in other parts of Sardinia tafonised rocks are referred to as *perdas perruntas* ('stones riddled with holes'). Sometimes mushroom-like structures form, for instance the so-called 'mushroom' (*fungo*) in Arzachena and the 'bear' (*orso*) at Capo d'Orso east of Palau. Traditionally *tafoni* are used by shepherds as natural shelters from sun and rain; it is not uncommon to find little walls built around them. *Tafoni* occur most frequently in granite, but can sometimes also be found with other types of rock.

*Photograph.
Bear Rock*

resort of **Cannigione** spread out along the beautiful, deeply-indented Golfo di Arzachena. Take the signposted left turn for BAIA SARDINIA (19km; the road ahead leads to Arzachena). When you meet a T-junction, turn left towards BAIA SARDINIA/PORTO CERVO. Then take the signposted right turn (28km) to PORTO CERVO/OLBIA not long before reaching the resort of Baia Sardinia. You get a brief glimpse of the small marina of Porto Quato on your left, snuggling in a narrow inlet.

Pass the turn-offs to Pitrizza and Liscia di Vacca before meeting a T-junction where you turn right for PORTO CERVO (signposted). Ignore the left turn for Porto Cervo Marina (33.5km), but turn left after some 300m to PORTO CERVO. Fork left on Via Stella Maris after another 150m, just where the road curves right. *(Watch out — this is a blind bend.)* Via Stella Maris leads you directly to the famous church of **Stella Maris** ('Star of the Sea'; ✝ 34km). Reminiscent of traditional Sardinian architecture, this modern church was built by Michele Busiri-Vicci in 1968. Continue to **Porto Cervo** (35km ▲▲▲✕➤), where you can park in the car park on your right. Follow the paved walkway from here down into the centre. Inhabited all year round, Porto Cervo is the exclusive main resort of the Costa Smeralda.

Continue ahead on the road, ignoring the signposted left turn to Porto Cervo Centro and passing more car parks. Meet the main road again and turn left to continue towards ARZACHENA/OLBIA. Then take the signposted left turn for OLBIA/CALA DI VOLPE. As the road winds downhill, you soon reach a road junction, where you first continue ahead towards ROMAZZINO/GOLF (the fork to the right is signposted for Olbia). After a short while you pass the classy Hotel Cala di Volpe (▲▲ 42km), one of the settings for the James Bond film 'The Spy Who Loved Me'. It was built in the style of a knight's castle by the French architect Jacques Couëlle in the 1960s. Some 400m beyond it (opposite the driveway to the Hotel Il Piccolo Golf), a track forks sharp right through the bushes to the sandy bay, from where there is a good view across the marina to the legendary hotel.

Return to the road junction (44.5km) and turn left for OLBIA/GOLFO ARANCI. A lay-by on the left (46.5km 📷) affords a splendid view of the seascape. Meet a T-junction (53km) and turn right towards SAN PANTALEO/ARZACHENA. Imposing serrated ridges dominate the landscape ahead; from a lay-by with a shrine on the right-hand side of the road you can enjoy the spectacular mountain scenery at leisure (57.5km 📷). Once in the centre of **San Pantaleo** (58.5km ✕➤), keep right towards ARZACHENA. The road now twists and bends downhill. On meeting a T-junction (62km), turn left to continue towards ARZACHENA. Soon go straight ahead for ARZACHENA, ignoring a right turn to Baia Sardinia. When you come to the main SS125 (64.5km), turn right for ARZACHENA. Two kilometres along, park in front of the **Museo Malchittu** (66.5km M✕) on your right, and break your journey with a short walk to the temple of Malchittu (see route description in the panel at the right).

Continue into the centre of **Arzachena** (69km ✕🚭⊕), where you take the signposted left turn for TEMPIO/CALANGIANUS/ LUOGOSANTO (Viale P Dettori) just beyond some traffic lights. Leave the town and keep ahead before taking the signposted right turn for TOMBA DEI GIGANTI CODDU VECCHIU (72km). Turn left after 2km (74km), to follow the signposted road for 400m to the visitor centre at the **Tomba dei Giganti Coddu Vecchiu★ (ⁿⁿM)**. This typical megalithic tomb was built in two distinct phases: an older corridor tomb (18-16C BC) was extended in Nuragic times (16-12C BC) by adding a semicircular forecourt *(exedra)* edged by stone slabs; this was used for cultic rites and sacrifices. The central stone slab or portal stone has a height of 4m/12ft; its edge is cut into the stone as a high relief. The small opening at the bottom of the portal stone gave the only access to the once-covered burial chamber. By the way: despite their name, these ancient people were no giants *(giganti)*, but quite short compared to the average height today; it was the monumental size of the tombs themselves that gave rise to the name in fairly recent times.

Return to the main road and turn left to continue. Then (77.5km) take the right turn signposted to LI LOLGHI/LI MURI. Keep on the main track as it bends slightly to the left (78.5km) and park just beside a large farm building (79.5km). Now follow the track to the left for a short walk (20 minutes return) to an interesting burial site dating from the late Neolithic period (3500-2700 BC). The track passes two farms, one on the right and the other on the left, before reaching the **Necropolis of Li Muri (ⁿ)**. Reminiscent of dolmen, this burial site comprises several rectangular tombs built of stone slabs. They are encircled by smaller stone slabs

Walk to the temple of Malchittu (Allow 40min return and an overall climb of 40m, 130ft) Follow the gated field track to the left of the museum. Soon go straight ahead past a farm on your right, ignoring another farm up on your left. Go through a gate and continue on the track as it begins to rise, passing a vineyard on the right. Go through another gate, followed by a short steep climb. Bear left at a fork in the track and soon turn left on a path running through scrub. The path climbs steeply over rocks, to reach the temple, standing on a small saddle. This rather plain drystone building features an apse at the back. It was probably built around 1500 BC and is well preserved except for the original wooden gable roof. A window over the lintel (architrave) serves to spread the weight.

Tomba dei Giganti Coddu Vecchiu

GIANTS' TOMBS

According to legend, giants with supernatural powers built the *nuraghi* and buried their dead in the so-called giants' tombs *(tomba dei giganti)*. In reality it was simply the enormous scale of these chamber tombs, built from stone slabs, which gave them their name. More than 500 giants' tombs have been found on Sardinia, the largest of which measure more than 30m/100ft in length. In these chamber tombs the Nuragic people kept the remains of their dead as in a charnel house.

Giants' tombs appear to be a further development of long dolmen and gallery graves. These were inspired by the western megalithic culture which radiated to Sardinia. At the front of a giants' grave two semicircular wall extensions embrace an *exedra*. If viewed from the air, these wall extensions look like horns, which is perhaps a reference to the cult of the bull. Older graves (before 1500 BC) have the *exedra* surrounded by huge upended stone slabs. The portal stone, which can be up to 4m/12ft high, is found in the centre; a small opening within the base provides access to the tomb itself.

standing in an upright position. They edged the earthen burial mounds *(tumuli)* that once covered each tomb. Beside each tomb, small stone boxes for sacrifices and several standing stones (menhirs) can be seen, some of which have fallen over.

Return to your car and continue ahead on the wide gravel track for 500m. Then leave your car in the car park on the left, to visit the **Tomba dei Giganti li Lolghi★** (80km 🏛). Dominated by its high portal stone, this fine megalithic tomb rises on a hillock. Apparently it was built by extending an existing chamber tomb (1800-1600 BC). It was once covered by a large elliptical burial mound *(tumulus)* some 27m/88ft long. It is therefore thought that all *tombe dei giganti* developed from more simple types of tombs such as chamber tombs and dolmens. As at Coddu Vecchiu, an edge is cut into the portal stone as a high relief — a masterpiece of its time.

Return to the asphalt road and turn right to continue. The tour now gradually leads into the interior of the Gallura, a scarcely populated mountainous region that seems unchanged from time immemorial. Granites glowing in white, yellow and reddish hues crop out in the entire northeastern

San Pietro delle Immagini (di Simbranos), near Bulzi

part of Sardinia, testifying to the crystalline base of the island. The landscape is characterised by long serrated ridges *(serras)*, seemingly endless cork oak woods and poor pastures. Scattered farms *(stazzi)* are seen now and then, a rare type of settlement on Sardinia. Immigrants from nearby Corsica settled in the Gallura beginning in the 17th century; they preferred to live in isolated *stazzi* rather than villages.

Reach a car park on the right (91km 🅿), from where steps climb over 100m/300ft to the ruined Castello di Balaiana (🏰) and the 12th-century Capella di San Leonardo (⛪). Continue ahead past the right turn to the Castello di Baldu (93km). Enter **Luogosanto** (95.5km) and follow signposting for TEMPIO through the village. Beyond Luogosanto the road winds down into a valley where you meet the SS133; turn left towards TEMPIO. The road gradually zigzags uphill before running dead straight across a plateau. You find yourself amidst a typical Gallurese landscape, scarcely populated and covered by light cork oak woods and pastures, with the granite *serras* of Aggius rising ahead.

Ignore the right turn to Agliento, but take the next right turn signposted to AGGIUS (115km). Then fork right again, following signposting for TRINTITÀ D'AGULTU/BADESI/VALLE

23

D'ORIA (117.5km). The road leads across another wide basin encircled by granite *serras*. Take the left turn signposted PANORAMICA DI AGGIUS (121km), now heading straight for the granite massif. Turn right when you meet a T-junction (123km). Soon there is a car park on the right (opposite a half-finished building), where you can enjoy the view (📷) of the bizarre granite rock formations at leisure. Some more lay-bys encourage short stops to admire this gorgeous mountain scenery. Down in a deep gully to the right is the Laghetto Santa Degna, a pond surrounded by a small park with picnic tables and benches (124km ⛩*P*1). Meet the village road when you enter **Aggius** and turn right to continue. There is a viewing platform on the left (125.5km 📷) affording a beautiful vista of the village, spread out on the foothills of its serrated granite ridges.

On coming to the SS127, turn left to **Tempio Pausania** (131km ✝⛰✖⛽⊕). Surrounded by mountains and evergreen oak woods, this is the friendly capital of the Gallura. The picturesque old town, with its traditional houses of grey, unplastered granite, still retains its historic ambience. Together with the neighbouring towns of Calangianus and Aggius, Tempio is the centre of the Sardinian cork industry.

Go straight ahead through the town in the direction of OLBIA until, just after crossing the railway, you can take the signposted right turn to OSCHIRI. Turn left at the next T-junction, soon leaving Tempio behind. The road winds its way gradually into wooded hills. You pass a signposted left turn to Monte Limbara/ Località Vallicciola (139km): this road zigzags up the slopes of Monte Limbara for 6.2km before reaching the Località Vallicciola,

Lago del Coghinas

where Walk 2 starts. The main tour, however, continues straight ahead on the SS392, soon passing a shady picnic spot called Fundu di Monti on the left, with stone benches and good spring water (140.5km ⛩). Following a valley, the road twists and bends steadily uphill through wooded mountains before crossing the **Passo del Limbara** (143km).

Now you descend in more bends. Eventually the Lago del Coghinas comes into sight. Ignore a right turn signposted to Coghinas soon before crossing the reservoir. When you reach the main SS199 trunk road just before **Oschiri** (163.5km), turn right towards SASSARI. Turn off right after 3km for CASTRO and meet a T-junction straight away: turn left towards TULA/ CASTRO. After well over 1km you reach the car park at the beautiful Romanesque pilgrimage church of **N S di Castro** (167.5km ✝*P*2; photograph page 15).

Return the same way to the main road and turn right to continue towards Sassari. Then take the signposted right turn towards MARTIS. Soon ignore the right turn for Tula and continue ahead towards CHIARAMONTI. Treeless pastureland extends all around you; a *nuraghe* rises prominently on a hillock to the right. The road gradually winds its way up to the trachyte plateau of Monte Sassu which rises ahead of you to the right; the slopes are studded with olive trees. When you reach the plateau, scattered cork oaks alternate with occasional fields; the imposing Limbara massif is seen rising in the distance.

Cross the SS672 before climbing in hairpin bends to the next plateau; this one is limestone. Bear left at the crossroads when you enter **Chiaramonti** (202km ✝♜✕⛽). Dominated by the ruined Castello dei Doria, the town is strategically situated on a limestone hill affording a splendid panorama of its surroundings. If you feel like stretching your legs, a short stroll will lead you through the narrow alleys of the old town up to the ruined castle, from where you enjoy a splendid view in all directions (*P*3). Down in the town there is a small shady park (⛩) on the right-hand side of the main road which is also a good place for a break. Continuing on the main road through the town, bear right downhill at a fork.

After a series of bends you reach the picturesque village of **Martis** (208.5km ✕), which is also set in a limestone region. At the end of the village, take the right turn signposted FORESTA PIETRIFICATA CARRUCANA 1 KM. Soon you reach a fork where you keep right, following the one-way system. The petrified trunks of juniper trees from the Tertiary period (photograph page 15) are scattered on a grassy hillside to your left, enclosed by a stone wall. Opposite there is a small fenced-in picnic site down by the river (*P*4; 210.5km). Continue to follow the one-way system, keeping left at the next fork. Meet your outward route again, and now turn right, back to the main road. Turn right again when you rejoin the main road (SS127).

Soon you cross under the railway; table-topped mountains rise all around you. Go through **Laerru** (220.5km) and continue ahead for 2km before turning left in the direction of CASTELSARDO. After another 2km, turn right down a concreted lane to the church shown on page 23, **San Pietro delle Immagini** (di Simbranos; 225km ✝). This beautiful country church stands isolated in a hollow. The white limestone walls alternating with reddish trachyte are a characteristic feature of Pisan late Romanesque style. Trachyte crops out in the surrounding depressions while the plateau is made of limestone — a stratification which is typical throughout the Anglona.

Continuing on the main road, the next village en route is **Bulzi**. Then the road climbs once more up onto a limestone plateau. When you enter Sedini a yellow signpost, 'Domus de Janas', points left to a rock with some cave dwellings. In the centre of **Sedini** (232.5km) there is a shady green space with benches. Continue ahead past a right turn at the end of the village. The SS143 leads across isolated plateaus in the direction of Castelsardo. Just before crossing the SS200, the Roccia dell'Elefante, shown below, rises on the right-hand side of the road. Shaped by wind and weather, this rock of trachyte and limestone bears a striking resemblance to an elephant when seen from the west. Cross the SS200 and continue ahead into **Castelsardo** (247km ✝ ▮ ▲ ▲ ✕ ▣ ⊕). Crowned by a ruined medieval castle which once belonged to the Genovese Doria family, the town is strategically placed on a rocky promontory jutting into the sea.

TOUR 2: BARBAGIA AND GENNARGENTU

Oliena • Orgosolo • Mamoiada • Fonni • Desulo • Aritzo • Gadoni • Seui • Monte Tonneri • Perda 'e Liana • Lanusei • Lotzorai • Santa Maria Navarrese • Baunei • Genna Croce • Genna Silana • Cala Gonone • Dorgali • Su Gologone • Oliena

323km/200mi; approximately 16 hours (two to three days)
En route: Picnics 5-7; Walks 3-15

Known as the Monti del Gennargentu, the highest massif on the island rises in eastern Sardinia. Still partly cloaked in native oak woods, the wide mountainous territory encircling the Gennargentu massif is referred to as the Barbagia — the 'barbarous' region, so christened by the ancient Romans because they never managed to conquer and civilise the indigenous tribes in these highlands. The economy is based on pastoral farming and wine-growing, the villages are few and far between. Many grey houses and new buildings with unplastered façades give these mountain villages a rather austere beauty. As well as excellent cheese, the famous red wine made from Cannonau grapes is produced in this region. To the east of the Gennargentu rises the adjoining Supramonte, an enormous limestone massif extending to the Golfo di Orosei where it fals away steeply along the coastline cliffs. Local customs and old traditions were alive in this isolated mountain range until the middle of the 20th century — when bandits were still up to mischief and the law was taken into one's own hands. The most ancient dialect of Sardinian is still spoken by the older generation in the Barbagia.

Crowned by glaring white crags, the imposing cliffs of the northwestern Supramonte rise southeast of Nuoro, the capital of the eponymous province. On their foothills lies the large farming community of **Oliena** (🏨 ✕ 🍴). Leave Oliena by heading south towards ORGOSOLO. At the end of the village you pass a left turn signposted to MACCIONE/ COOP. ENIS: this would take you up to the starting point for Walk 3. Continue ahead on the main road, twisting and bending along the foothills of the Supramonte.

Once a notorious stronghold of bandits, **Orgosolo** (18km ✕ 🍴) nowadays sees whole busloads of tourists flooding the village. They are attracted by the famous wall paintings that are created by local and foreign artists alike (photograph overleaf). Depicting political and social issues, the inscriptions are often written in Sardinian. Most of these *murales* are seen on the houses along the main road as you drive through the village. Continue straight ahead towards

Murals at Orgosolo

Mamoiada. The main road leads in a series of bends to **Mamoiada** (29km ✕🍽). This village is famous for the expressive wood-carved masks that are worn at carnival time by eerily-costumed shepherds *(mamuthones)*.

When you reach the fork at the end of the village, keep left for FONNI. The road winds its way through partly-wooded hills, eventually passing a left turn to Prato Bello and crossing under the main SS389 trunk road immediately afterwards. Situated at 1000m/3300ft above sea level, **Fonni** (45km ▲✕🍽) is the highest village on Sardinia. Keep left at the main road junction in the village. Turn right shortly after leaving the last houses behind, now heading straight for the highest mountains on Sardinia. You pass a left turn signposted to MONTE SPADA/BRUNCU SPINA (51km); it leads to the only ski resort on the island.*

The road tortuously rounds the isolated valley of the Riu Aratu before reaching a crossroads at a pass, the **Arcu de Tascussi** (1245m/4085ft; 64km; several signposts; bar; ♦🍴). Here you could turn left to the starting point of Walk 11, but the main route continues straight ahead. Not far beyond the pass, there is a picnic spot with a well on the right (🍴). The road slowly winds down to **Desulo** (70km ▲✕🍽) and leads through this drawn-out village via the main street.

*If you have time, take this turn for a scenic detour of 24km return. Keep right at a fork after 1km. You will reach the Funtana Ervarisciu after another 4km — just a well by a wall. Next comes the Funtana Massiai with a stone bench and seats, reached after a further 2km; trees offer some shade. Soon the narrow lane crosses the Genna Luddurreo. Now the view opens up to the east over desolate mountains. The lane eventually passes another well before it ends at the valley station of a chairlift.

When you meet the SS295 further down in the valley, turn left for BELVI/ARITZO, soon crossing the narrow-gauge railway. After a short while you can glimpse a beautiful viaduct on your left. The road snakes through lush woodland to **Belvi** (84km ✕▣M). Go through the village, keeping left at the fork, towards ARITZO.

The friendly mountain village of **Aritzo**, starting point for Walks 12-14, is quickly reached (87km ▲▲✕▣M; photograph page 98). Aritzo became a popular summer resort in the early 1900s — not least because these airy heights were less endangered by malaria than the marshy lowlands (see panel page 90). Go straight ahead through the village. Leaving the last houses behind, turn left for GADONI at the crossroads opposite the Cantoniera Cossatzu. Soon a splendid view of Gadoni opens up, with its houses clinging to the slopes of the deeply-carved Tistigliosi Valley. There is a well in a shady wall on the left just before you enter **Gadoni** (97km ✕▣).

Beyond the village, the road describes a series of tortuous bends as it winds down into the Flumendosa Valley. This imposing ravine-like valley is backed by sheer limestone cliffs *(tonneris)*. You cross a high modern bridge. As you gradually approach the *tonneris*, the immediate landscape looses its Mediterranean character and takes on a 'Wild West' aspect. You come upon a featureless limestone plateau covered with *garrigue* and edged with *tonneris*.

You pass the chapel of San Pietro (109km ✝) on the right and, almost immediately, a beautiful view opens up towards Seulo, with its houses clinging to the steep hillside. At the entrance to the village there is a shady picnic area to the right (▤). Go through **Seulo** (111km ✕▣); just after passing the Carabinieri there is another shady green space on the right where you could picnic (▤). Leave the village behind and pass a well (114km ▤). Not far beyond the Cantoniera Gennauassa (117km), a sign points left to a *sorgente* (spring) in a shady wood (▤). The road has just taken you in a series of bends through wooded hill country but, all of a sudden, you reach a gaunt plateau framed by typical Sardinian mountain ranges. Vine are grown here in some areas — at an altitude of 800m/2400ft!

Take the signposted right turn to the **Grotta de is Janas** (122km café/✕▤) and, after your visit, return to the main road and turn right to continue, crossing the railway line straight away. At the T-junction with the SS198, turn left for Seui. A series of bends follows, then you cross under the railway line. The hillsides to your right plunge down to the deeply-carved Sadali Valley. You pass the small picturesque railway station before reaching **Seui** (133km ✕🍴), a village situated on a steep hill overlooking the Sadali Valley.

Beyond the village, the SS198 continues on its tortuous way. Ignore the first turn on your left after 5km (signposted to Monte Tonneri/Perda Liana) and continue on the main road. Pass the **Cantoniera Arcueri** after another 4km (142km) and turn left for PERDA LIANA/MONTARBU/LAGO ALTO FLUMENDOSA just 100m beyond it. Almost immediately, there is a chapel on your left and a small picnic area on your right (🍴). Keep to the small asphalt lane; to your left there is a sweeping view over a treeless and somewhat bleak landscape. After 5km on this lane, the road from Seui joins from the left. Another 2km along, you come to a right turn signposted CASERMA MONTARBU 11 KM (149km). The main tour continues ahead at this junction, but you have the option of making a detour (21km return) to the Foresta Demaniale Montarbu/Monte Tonneri (🍴P5; Walk 15).

Carry straight on along the asphalt lane, ignoring a left turn (155km). Soon a splendid vista unfolds before you, out over the deeply-carved Flumendosa Valley, with the Gennargentu massif rising in the background. The river itself is not seen from up here. To the left, the **Nuraghe Ardasai** (155.5km) stands proudly on a nose of rock overlooking the valley; it almost seems as if this megalithic tower is growing out of the rock. There is also a good view of the sheer rocky escarpment of Monte Tonneri and the prominent pinnacle of Perda 'e Liana.

The road twists and bends along the northern buttress of **Monte Tonneri**. You pass a well (157.5km) where you can fill your bottles with fresh spring water. Take the signposted right turn PERDA LIANA 0,6 (168km) and follow the road uphill for 800m before stopping where a gravel track forks sharp left. Leave your car here for a short leg-stretcher to the foot of nearby **Perda 'e Liana**. The gravel track leads within 100m to a parking area just before a bridge. Go through the wooden gate beyond it (or cross the stile beside it), following the footpath to Perda 'e Liana.

Continue to drive through isolated hills. Turn sharp left when you reach a crossroads (173.5km). Then take the signposted right turn for SARCEREI and cross the narrow-gauge railway on a bridge. The road snakes uphill, initially through woods sadly devastated by fire, then through beautiful mixed woodland. Ignore a left turn to the Osservatorio astronomico (184.5km). The road gradually begins to descend. Meet the SS198 (186.5km) and turn left down to **Lanusei** (194.5km ⛰✕🚱⊕). About 1km beyond the town centre, take the right turn to TORTOLI/ ILBONO, soon crossing the railway. At the T-junction in **Ilbono** (197.5km), turn right for TORTOLI. The SS198 twists and bends down into the fertile coastal plain of the Ogliastra.

Ignore the left turn for Villagrande and continue ahead towards TORTOLI. Join the main SS125 trunk road shortly before reaching Tortoli and head north towards OLBIA/ OROSEI. The mountain village of Baunei and the Supramonte are seen ahead of you in the distance. Just after crossing the Riu Girasole, the castle rock of Lotzorai (also called Castello di Medusa) is seen on your left. Continue straight ahead through **Lotzorai** (218.5km) before crossing the Riu Pramaera. Then take the signposted right turn to **Santa Maria Navarrese** (222.5km ✝⛰🏠✕🚱), where Walk 10 ends. This friendly coastal village (nowadays a resort) began to develop around a pilgrimage church. Surrounded by ancient olive trees, this plain building dates back to the 11th century. Legend has it that the church was donated by a daughter of the king of Navarra when she was shipwrecked off the coast but was happily saved from danger.

Landscape near Oliena

KARSTIFICATION

The limestone massifs of Sardinia, including the Supramonte and the Nurra, are strongly *karstified*. (Karst is the German name for a mountain range east of Trieste, but the term is now generally applied to all mountains exhibiting such erosion of limestone and dolomite.) Under certain conditions, these two types of rock are sparingly soluble in water, so over long periods of time they can be dissolved by rain water.

The first surface indications of this process are grooves or holes. In addition, rainwater penetrates the rock through gaps and fissures, dissolving it from inside, while leaving the external massif largely intact. The hollows which are created eventually grow into extensive cave systems. At that stage very little rainwater runs along the surface; most of it is immediately swallowed via holes and chasms into the cave system. The caves open into the valleys and along the edges of the mountains, for instance on the Gulf of Orosei. Where the caves carry water, strong springs like the Sorgente de su Gologne have their source. However, the water can dissolve only small amounts of calcium carbonate (the main constituent of limestone). In saturated solutions,

some of the dissolved calcium carbonate is easily redeposited. Over millennia, the equilibrium between dissolving and re-depositing of calcium carbonate creates caves with fantastically formed stalactites and stalagmites. These are sometimes called dripstone formations because water is the active substance.

Photograph: karstified rock in the Supramonte

Turn left at the main road junction in the village. Soon rejoin the SS125 and turn right for **Baunei** (232.5km ✕🚐), the starting point for Walk 10 (*P*6 and Walk 9 are nearby). Beyond Baunei, the road winds across several passes, affording magnificent views of the fertile Ogliastra with its colourful tapestry of fields and pastures. Twisting and bending, you thread your way between the limestone massif of the Supramonte. Ignore the left turn (252.5km) for Urzulei, where Walk 8 begins. Soon you pass the **Genna Croce** (255.5km; bar), starting point for Walk 7.

Leading through some galleried tunnels, the SS125 continues through isolated mountains covered mainly in oaks. When you reach the **Genna Silana** (261km ✕📷), you enjoy a first wide view to the Valle di Oddoene. On the western flanks of this wide flat-bottomed valley, the enormous cleft of the Gola su Gorropu splits the limestone massif. Affording panoramic views all along, the road continues through magnificent mountain scenery, but there are few places where you can stop safely to admire the views. The first good stop is at the **Casa Cantoniera Bidicolai** (267.5km 📷), a derelict road keepers' house. Some 2km past another house on the left (269km), a gravel track forks off sharp left (271km) to the starting point for Walk 5.

Then you pass the access road off left to Walk 4 (279km). Continue for another kilometre before taking the right turn (280km) to CALA GONONE. Go through a tunnel cut through the limestone ridge and, at the exit, stop immediately in the car park on the left (⊞). A stunning seascape unravels quite unexpectedly, as the high limestone ridges of the Supra-monte massif open out like a natural amphitheatre to frame the azure Golfo di Orosei. There is a sweeping view over green holm oaks and olive trees down to the resort of Cala Gonone on the coast. The road descends in hairpin bends to **Cala Gonone** (287.5km ▲▲▲✕⊞; Walk 6). Originally founded as a small harbour for merchant shipping at the end of the 18th century, Cala Gonone became a popular seaside resort 100 years ago.

Return through the tunnel to the SS125 and continue north. Bear right when you reach the fork at the entrance to **Dorgali**, following the upper bypass; it affords a nice view over the rooftops (296.5km). Leave your car by the roadside and stroll down into the old town. The SS125 leads you out of Dorgali and downhill across a basalt plateau, with the rocky flanks of the Supramonte rising in the west. Take the signposted left turn for NUORO/OLIENA. The road soon crosses the Lago del Cedrino on a high bridge. Far below you, some sections of the old road which crossed the river valley before this reservoir was flooded, can still be seen.

Soon turn left for OLIENA/NUORO. (But those of you keen on archaeology can first continue straight ahead for 2.5km towards Orosei, until Serra Orrios is signposted on your right — a very well preserved Nuragic village complete with two megaron temples.)

The main route continues towards the rocky cliffs of the Supramonte. After about 8km you reach a sharp turn on your left (312.5km), signposted to the HOTEL SU GOLOGONE. Take it and follow this narrow country lane straight ahead. After 2km you pass the drive up to this high-class hotel. Ignore a concrete road turning off right after another 200m and continue ahead to the large car park on the leafy banks of the river Cedrino (314.5km). Behind and below the chapel of N S della Pieta, the spring of **Su Gologone** (the largest spring on Sardinia) pours out from a deep cleft in the karst rock, with its water shimmering in almost unreal turquoise hues. There are some picnic tables and benches on the shady river bank (⊞P7).

Return the way you came and turn left on rejoining the main road. Ignore a right turn to Nuoro and continue straight back into **Oliena** (323km).

TOUR 3: MARMILLA AND SARCIDANO

Laconi • Nurri • Orroli • Santa Vittoria • Serri • Isili • Nurallao • Gesturi • Barumini • Las Plassas • Tuili

134km/83mi; approximately 6 hours (one day)
En route: Picnic 8; Picnic 9 is nearby; Walk 16

Varied landscapes and some pretty market towns are featured on this tour. Some masterpieces of Nuragic architecture wait for you: an imposing tower bastion, an important sanctuary and a megalithic tomb. The basalt plateau of Giara di Gesturi, a windswept plain rising in the fertile Marmilla region, is famous for its semi-wild horses roaming the sparse cork oak woods.

Head north from **Laconi** (✖🍽) on the SS128 until you can take the right turn for SANTA SOFIA. This road runs across the isolated and barren plateau of the Sarcidano; it's not surprising to find a prison *(colonia penale)* here. Below Villanovatulo (31km) meet the SS198 and turn right. There is a beautiful view to the east over the elongated Lago del Flumendosa. A short time later you cross the narrow-gauge railway and wind your way up the steep flanks of a plateau. Soon after recrossing the railway, take the signposted left turn for NURRI/ORROLI/NURAGHE ARRUBIU (by a well; 🅿). The road runs across another gaunt plateau to **Nurri** (50km ✖🍽). When you leave the village, there is a promenade with some benches on your right, affording a good view out over the rolling hills of the Marmilla (photograph page 55).

The next village en route is **Orroli** (52.5km). Bear right at the fork in the village for ALAPLANO/URGUSDONIGALA. After some 100m you reach a junction where you keep left on the main road, following signposting for the NURAGHE ARRUBIU. Continue ahead out of the village, then take the signposted left turn to the *nuraghe*. This asphalt lane runs across gaunt grazing land criss-crossed by stone walls. Keep left at a fork; now the imposing **Nuraghe Arrubiu** (59.5km 🎟) rises ahead of you.

When you have visited the complex, return the same way via Orroli and Nurri to the SS198 and turn left towards ISILI. Meet the SS128 and turn left towards the SANTUARIO NURAGHICO SANTA VITTORIA. After 1km take the sharp right fork that leads you into **Serri**. Keep left in the village, following the same signposting. Leave Serri and continue across the narrow plateau of Sa Giara to the car park at the Nuragic sanctuary of **Santa Vittoria**★ (86km 🎟P8). From the visitor centre, follow the gravel track straight ahead for a few minutes, until it swings right. The chapel of Santa Vittoria stands just at the steep cliff-edge of the plateau; in front of

it is the sacred place with the famous holy well shown at the right.

Return the same way to the main road in **Serri** (91.5km) and follow it to the left. There is a small green space with seats by the village church from where you enjoy a nice view to the east. Leaving the village, a series of hairpin bends leads you down off the plateau. You cross the railway line and meet the SS128. Turn left for Isili; a prominent table-top mountain rises ahead of you. Keep right on the main road in **Isili** (99km ✕🍴), following signposting for Laconi. Take the signposted left turn to the Nuraghe Is Paras just past the police headquarters (Carabinieri). Cross the railway and park next to the sports stadium, by the enclosed area. The well-preserved **Nuraghe Is Paras** (🏛; title page photograph) sits prominently on a hill.

Continue ahead or the walled asphalt lane when you have visited the complex. Soon there is a view of a small reservoir fed by the Riu Mannu. Bear right at a fork, rejoin the SS128, and turn left to continue. Two bridges lead across arms of the reservoir; a ruined chapel lies on an islet. Pass a small country church (✝) on the left before reaching **Nurallao** (106.5km ✕🍴). Take the signposted left turn (SS197) for Nuragus when you enter the village. Just past the Agip petrol station, turn left on a gravel road (yellow signposting: Tomba megalitica Aiodda 2 km) for a detour to this famous Megalithic tomb. After 400m fork left on the tarred field track. After another 1.3km you reach a signposted left turn by an imposing fig tree. Leave your car here and follow the field track for about 200m until it forks. Turn right and follow this track

HOLY WELLS

Water has great significance in several of the Mediterranean cultures. In the Nuragic period, water deities had the highest status, and nearly all places of worship were located by wells or springs. More than 50 holy wells, all built in a similar way, are known on Sardinia today. Typically, one enters an antechamber, with stone benches on either side on which offerings like the famous Sardinian bronze statuettes illustrated on page 126 were displayed. From there, steps lead down to the well room, which was covered by a dome and looked like a small *nuraghe*. Many holy wells are architectural masterpieces. For example, the walls of the holy sanctuary of Santa Cristina (Car tour 5) consist of very precisely cut rectangular blocks of stone. Each layer protrudes slightly more than the one below; thus the walls form a fascinating dog-tooth profile, and there is a great sense of depth.

Photograph: holy well at Santa Vittoria (Picnic 8)

SU NURAXI

The massive fortress of Su Nuraxi rises on the foothills of the Giara di Gesturi, not far from the friendly farming village of Barumini. The complex was started around 1500 BC and later extended several times. The central tower has an impressive dome, which is nearly 8m/25ft high on the lower level. It is the oldest part of the complex and surrounded by four other towers and a ring wall. The central courtyard features a well 20m/65ft deep. The bastion was later surrounded by a wider ring wall with seven turrets. In front of the fortress one can see the remains of walls from a Nuragic village comprising over 200 round huts, which were probably originally covered with tree trunks, twigs and leaves. The largest round hut has a small circular stone bench along the inner wall and presumably served as a place where the people congregated

*Photograph:
Su Nuraxi*

uphill, crossing another track diagonally to the left after three minutes. Continue on the field track for another four minutes until the enclosed **Tomba megalitica Aiodda** (∏) comes up on your right.

Return the same way to the main SS197 and turn left. The Giara di Gesturi, Sardinia's largest table mountain, rises ahead of you. Ignore the right turn to Genoni in **Nuragus** (113.5km). Pass through the pretty farming village of **Gesturi** (119.5km) and continue on the SS197. Turn right on the bypass when you enter **Barumini** (▲ ✕ 🖵). Turn right again at the main crossroads in the village. Soon you reach the car park at the famous Nuragic fortress of **Su Nuraxi★** on the left, now included in the UNESCO World Heritage List (125km ∏; café/✕ opposite). The castle mountain of Las Plassas, resembling a volcanic cone, rises in the south, while rolling hills are seen in all directions. From Su Nuraxi return to the main crossroads in **Barumini** (126km) and turn right for LAS PLASSAS.

In **Las Plassas** (129km) take the signposted right turn for the CASTELLO, the sparse remains of a ruined castle, once a stronghold of the judges of Arborea. Overlooking the entire Marmilla, the position of the castle was strategically well chosen. When you meet a T-junction at the foot of the steep conical mound crowned by the castle (■), turn right, passing an interesting old church (✝) on the right. The edge of the Giara di Gesturi is seen rising ahead of you to the right, while rolling hills slope away to the left. At another T-junction, turn left into **Tuili** (134km ✕ 🖵), then refer to page 108, to reach the car park on the Giara di Gesturi (**P**9; Walk 16). This unique basalt plateau, with its lakes and wild horses roaming about freely, can only be explored on foot.

TOUR 4: SULCIS AND IGLESIENTE

Cagliari • Pula • Chia • Santadi • Giba • Sant' Antioco • Calasetta • Nebida • Iglesias • Fluminimaggiore • Arbus - Montevecchio • Gutturu e Flumini • Guspini • Terralba - Arborea • Oristano

349km/216mi; approximately 17 hours (three days)

En route: Picnic 10; Walks 17 and 20; Walks 18 and 19 are nearby.

Separated from the rest of Sardinia by the Cixerri rift valley, the southwest of the island comprises two great mountain ranges cloaked in dense oak woods, the Iglesiente and Sulcis. Occasional spoil heaps, abandoned miners' villages, and old mine shafts and galleries bear witness to the past, when this region was extensively mined for silver, lead, zinc, iron ores and many other minerals; the richest mines in the whole of Italy are found here. Today it is a landscape of great scenic splendour, with good trails snaking through the hills and stunning vistas from the mountaintops. You also come upon magnificent seascapes with glorious sandy beaches, archaeological sites dating from Phoenician times, enormous limestone caverns with dripstone formations and flocks of flamingos wading through the lagoons.

Leave **Cagliari** (✝■▲✕⛽⊕) in a westerly direction, following signposting for Pula/Teulada. The SS195 sweeps through the Stagno di Cagliari, the biggest lagoon on Sardinia. Despite many industrial plants, it is a haven for water fowl and migrating birds. Large flocks of flamingos can be seen here seasonally, wading through the brackish water in search of food, quite undisturbed by the traffic. The expressway bypasses Sarroch with its big petrochemical complex. Soon you pass Villa San Pietro and continue on the country road into **Pula** (31.5km ▲✕⛽). Signposting leads you through the town to the Phoenician site of **Nora★** (35km П), situated at the tip of a narrow neck of land. The church of Sant' Efisio (✝) stands near the large car park. Every year at the beginning of May, this church is the destination of a big procession that starts out in Cagliari.

Return to Pula and continue on the SS195 towards TEULADA. The road runs dead straight past some hotels (▲) hidden in pine groves before crossing the Arcu de Generuxi. Soon take the signposted left turn to **Chia** (55.5km), little more than a crossroads with a bar and a supermarket by the roadside. You could make a detour to the beaches at the Torre di Chia by bearing left here (1.8km return), but the tour heads straight on, passing more forks leading to the magnificent sandy beaches along the Costa del Sud. An old lighthouse rises at the Capo Spartivento.

Leave the coastal plain of Chia with its lagoons *(stagni)* behind. Shortly after crossing a low saddle at the Punta Pinnetta, watch for a small holiday camp with two entrance gates on the left (61km); this is where Walk 17 begins. The road winds along the Costa del Sud. Occasional lay-bys allow you to stop and admire the splendid views (📷; photograph page 114) at leisure. A short detour to the signposted SPIAGGA TUERREDDA (62km) is worth the trip. The road rounds a bay and affords beautiful views of the old watchtower on Capo Malfatano. Then there is a sweeping vista over the Golfo di Teulada, backed to the west by the Capo Teulada, the most southerly point on Sardinia.

The road swings inland and runs (past a turn-off to the Porto di Teulada) straight back to the SS195. Turn right, continuing in the direction of TEULADA. On the outskirts of **Teulada**, almost immediately after passing a petrol station (⛽), fork left for SANTADI/GROTTE IS ZUDDAS. The road twists and bends through the hills, passing the hamlet of **Is Carillus** and the signposted right turn to the GROTTE IS ZUDDAS (95.5km). If you have time, it's worth visiting this limestone cavern with its wonderful dripstone formations and unusual crystalline formations. Continue past some small hamlets to **Santadi** (102km ✕⛽). Follow the road towards IGLESIAS until you meet the SS293, where you turn left to **Giba** (112km ✕).

Go straight through the village. Less than 4km past Giba, take the right turn to **Tratalias** (120.5km ♣). Here you meet a T-junction were the tour will continue to the left, but first turn right to the churchyard which is dominated by the fine Romanesque village church. Then head west, quickly leaving the village behind. Cross the SS195 and meet the SS126. Turn left, heading for SANT' ANTIOCO. Crossing a dam and passing near an old Roman bridge, you reach the island of **Sant' Antioco** with its eponymous main town (135km ♣⛰✕⛽). Continue on the SS126^{dir} to **Calasetta** (144.5km), a small harbour from where the ferry to the island of San Pietro departs.

Return to the SS126 and follow it north past Carbonia, a mining town built in the 1930s under Mussolini's regime for quarrying brown coal (lignite). Some 100m before passing the northern access road to Carbonia, you reach an inconspicuous fork by some houses on your left which is signposted to the ACROPOLI DI MONTE SIRAI. Turn left here, then right straight away (signposted) and follow the road up to the **Acropoli di Monte Sirai** (174km 🏛). This Phoenician site lies prominently on a basalt table-top mountain that drops off steeply on all sides.

NORA

Situated at the end of a narrow headland, Nora is regarded as the oldest town on Sardinia. Even in Nuragic times there was a settlement here, as can be seen by the Nuragic well and some other remains. In Punic and, later, Roman times, Nora flourished as a port. Depending on the direction of the wind, ships could steer into one of three harbours — all of which have now disappeared into the sea. The few remains from Phoenician/Punic times include the Aesculapian temple on the south-western tip and the crowded residential area to the west of the theatre, with its bathtub-like cisterns. The town was almost entirely rebuilt under the Romans. They created several thermal baths with beautiful mosaics and a small, well-preserved theatre. The four large clay vessels in the basement of the stage building probably served as sound amplifiers. The town had tidily-cobbled streets with an elaborate sewage system. During the period of the Roman emperors, two grand residential buildings were erected, their atriums lined by columns.

Photographs: Roman mosaic floor at Nora (left) and the San Remy Bastion at Cagliari (right)

Return downhill the same way. Rejoin the SS126 and turn left, continuing north. Then take the signposted left turn to NEBIDA/MASUA and follow this road to the large car park in **Nebida** (194km). Here you can stretch your legs by following the signposted belvedere circuit that begins at the car park, a walkway affording splendid views of the multi-coloured cliffs along the coast and the old mining facilities. Then return to the SS126 and turn left to continue. The road runs through the enormous mining district of Monteponi before you take the first exit into **Iglesias** (208km ⚓🏛🏔 ✕🏤⊕). Founded by the Pisans as a mining centre and the seat of a bishopric in the 12th century, Iglesias ('churches') grew mainly during the industrial revolution when the surrounding Iglesiente was the most important mining region in the whole of Italy. The charming old town with its maze of narrow alleys merits a visit.

Continue north on the SS126, quickly leaving the town behind and crossing the Lago Corsi. The road twists and bends uphill through wooded countryside. Shortly after crossing the **Arcu Genna Bogai**, you pass a group of houses called **Sant' Angelo** (219.5km 🏕 bar) that date from the foundation of a small monastery. Take a break here, enjoying the fresh mountain air ... and a good cup of cappuccino!

Not much further on, take the signposted right turn (222.5km) to the **Tempio di Antas** (225km ℹ). The asphalt road ends at a car park in front of the fenced-in site, where Walk 20 begins (photograph page 126). After visiting the Phoenician/Roman temple, return to the SS126 and continue north. Watch for an inconspicuous turn on your left less than 5km along the SS126 (232km) that leads to the GROTTA SU MANNU (∏P10). If you haven't already visited this fine limestone cavern on Walk 20, here is another opportunity: a short detour (2.8km return) will take you to the car park. The main tour continues north on the SS126.

Beyond **Fluminimaggiore** (236km ✕🏪), the high oak forest gives way to scrubby *macchia*. Ignoring several turn-offs, follow the convoluted SS126 to **Arbus** (255.5km ✕🏪). Take a sharp left turn near the end of this village (shortly before reaching the cemetery), following signposting to the COSTA VERDE. At the junction in **Montevecchio** (262.5km), bear right to the Costa Verde. Follow this road as it twists and bends in a northwesterly direction through isolated hill country. Then take the signposted left turn down to **Gutturu e Flumini** on the **Costa Verde** (278km).

From here you could follow the coastal road for another 7.5km along the Costa Verde which is famous for its golden sand dunes. But the tour turns back and leads via Montevecchio to **Guspini** (301.5km ✕🏪). Meet the SS126 in the town and turn left in the direction of ORISTANO. The road runs north in a dead straight line via San Nicolo to **Terralba** (321.5km). Turn left here and continue to **Arborea** (331km). This agricultural community with its scattered farms was founded in the 1920s after the marshy coastal flats had been drained; farmers from Northern Italy were settled here.

The tour continues north on the SS126 past two lagoons, the Ena Arrubia and the Stagno di Santa Giusta, before you finally reach **Oristano** (349km 🏕🏔✕🏪⊕).

TOUR 5: SINIS PENINSULA, MONTE FERRU AND LAGO OMODEO

Oristano • Tharros • Cuglieri • San Leonardo de Siete Funtes • Nuraghe Losa • Santa Cristina • Zuri • Tadasuni • Sorradile • Ortueri • Busachi • Fordongianus • Oristano

232km/144mi; approximately 11 hours (two days)
En route: Picnics 11-14

Tharros is the most famous Phoenician settlement on Sardinia and will fire you with enthusiasm even if you are not an archaeology buff. Equally impressive are the buildings dating back to the Nuragic civilisation, of which you will see a well-preserved tower and a sanctuary. The enormous volcano of Monte Ferru provides another highlight. You also come upon some lovely country villages and fine churches as you travel through pleasant countryside.

From **Oristano** (♀♠✕🍴⊕) follow the SS292 north towards TORRE GRANDE/CUGLIERI, crossing the Tirso Valley on a long bridge when you reach the outskirts. Keep left at two forks, following CABRAS/THARROS. Soon the beautiful church of Madonna di Rimedio (♀) is seen on the right. Now follow signposting for SAN GIOVANNI DI SINIS; you first come into **Torre Grande** (9km), where you take the first right turn at the big roundabout. Soon meet a T-junction and turn left towards SAN GIOVANNI DI SINIS. The large Stagno di Cabras is now on your right, the Stagno di Mistras on the left. Continue ahead past a right turn towards Tharros. Beyond the Romanesque church on the left in **San Giovanni di Sinis** (♀), the road ends at the Phoenician site of **Tharros★** (22.5km ♣; see panel overleaf). An old watchtower stands guard on the headland; the coast is hemmed by lovely sandy beaches.

Return the same way until you can take the signposted left turn to SAN SALVATORE/RIOLA. This road leads past the

Sinis Peninsula near Tharros

THARROS

Located on a promontory at the Gulf of Oristano, the ruins of Tharros still bear witness to its origin as a Phoenician-Punic trading town, although much of Tharros, like Nora, was later rebuilt by the Romans.

Items of interest include the Punic pseudo-portico temple, thermal baths, temples, theatres, and the foundation walls of Roman houses.

Tharros started to lose importance during the time of the Roman emperors; even its elevation to a bishopric could not change this. From late classical antiquity onwards the city was often ransacked by Vandals and Saracens. For this reason — and also because of the danger of malaria (see panel page 90) — Tharros was abandoned around 1000 AD and relocated further inland, where the new town of Oristano was founded.

hamlet of **San Salvatore** with its eponymous church. Continue ahead, ignoring the left turn for Is Arutas shortly beyond it. There is a sweeping view to the right over the wide expanse of the Stagno di Cabras. Go ahead past another left turn (to Putzu Idu/Sa Rocca Tunda). Soon a *nuraghe* comes into view close by on your right. Monte Ferru rises further inland to the northeast. Artichokes, tomatoes, grapes, wheat and melons are cultivated in the surrounding fields.

Meet the SS292 and turn left towards CUGLIERI. Nuraghe Tradori rises prominently on the right. Reach the pleasant resort of **Torre del Pozo** (53km), with its houses gathering round a bay. Built to defend the coastline against corsair attacks, the ancient Torre su Pattu rises on the headland. The resort of S'Architettu follows straight away. The next resort on the coast is **Santa Caterina di Pittinuri** (57km). Dominated by the Torre Pittinuri, it also snuggles in a small bay. Behind the beach there is a shady picnic area in a small valley (⊼*P*11). As Cuglieri gradually draws nearer, the volcanic massif of Monte Ferru rises imposingly on the right, culminating in craggy hilltops. Its upper slopes are densely wooded, while olive groves are spread out on the foothills.

In the centre of **Cuglieri** (72.5km ✕🍽), take the right turn for SANTU LUSSURGIU. The road winds uphill in a series of deep hairpin bends. These heights are densely wooded and the air is fresh — what a contrast to the flat and gaunt Sinis Peninsula! Quite unexpectedly, a cobbled footpath on the right climbs up to the ruined Castello di Monte Ferru (Etzu;

75 5km ■); there is a lay-by on the right (2-3 cars) 5⊃m
be⊂re a small bridge with rusty white railings, where the
foo⊂path begins. You pass a shady picnic area (79km ⊟P12;
sp⁃ ng with delicious fresh water) and a shrine on a rock
af⁃er another 2km. Ignore a right turn some 300m beyond
th⁼ shrine, and the right turn up to the top of Monte Ferru.

As the road reaches its highest point, a splendid p⌐no-
ra⊓a unravels, stretching from north to south across the
c⁼ntral highlands of Sardinia and various plateaus. Soon
t⌐⟨e the signposted left turn to **San Leonardo de Siete Fures**
(⊟8.5km ⊟P13), and leave your car by the circular fountain.
⁻⁼ere is a shady park to the left above the road, with seven
bubbling springs ('S⁃ete Funtes'). The surroundings,
⊃omewhat neglected, are wild and romantic, with ivy
⊂reeping up the gnarled old trees. Go up the track by the
⟨ellow signs (SORGENTI/CHIESA ROMANICA SAN LEONARDO),
then go right to the little Romanesque trachyte church,
⁻eaturing a cross of the Knights of St John (⚓).

Return to the main road and turn left to continue. Pass a
shady picnic area on the right, where a spring delivers fresh
drinking water (92.5km ⊟). Meet a T-junction (95km) and
turn left for ABBASANTA (a right turn would take you into Santu
Lussurgiu). You are now descending to the pl⌐teau of
Abbasanta, with the central highlands rising ahead of you
in the distance. The barren plain is dotted with large heaps
of stones. Eventually scattered cork oaks begin to appear
and you pass the hamlet of **Sant' Agostino** (104.5km).

Join the motorway and go south towards C⌐gliari for
1km, until the signposted turn to the **Nuraghe Losa★** comes
on your right (111km ⌂). After you have visited this famous
fortress, continue south on the motorway, then take the
signposted exit to the Nuragic sanctuary of **Santa Cristina★**
(120km ⌂; bar; see panel on page 35).

When you have visited the site, drive back north on the
motorway before bearing right near Abbasanta towards
NUORO/OLBIA. Then take the first exit and follow signposting
to **Ghilarza** (132km ✕⛾). Follow signs for SORRADILE through
the town, passing an Aragonese tower adjacent to a chapel.
Very reminiscent of sandstone, every building in this town
is made of reddish trachyte which is of volcanic origin. Cross
the motorway and take the left turn to SODDI/ZURI straight
away. Then fork right for ZURI; there is a sweeping view on
the left out over the Lago Omodeo. Flooded in the 1920s,
this is the largest reservoir on Sardinia. There is a beautiful
trachyte church on the left just where you enter **Zuri**
(137.5km ⚓). Continue straight ahead from Zuri.

Soon you reach a major crossroads where you turn left for **Tadasuni** (140km ✝). Here the houses are built of black volcanic rock, which gives the village a quite different character. The Museo degli instrumenti della musica popolare sarde is worth a visit (**M**; only by appointment; contact Giovanni Dore, tel. 0785/50113). Pass the right turn to the Diga Tirso and wind down into the Tirso Valley with its reservoir, crossing it on a huge bridge. At a fork, keep left on the main road, to reach **Sorradile** (147.5km). This picturesque village is characterised by houses built of red trachyte. There are good views of the Lago Omodeo as the road winds up to **Nughedu Santa Vittoria** (150.5km). Go straight ahead through this village towards AUSTIS/NEONELI.

You are now climbing a plateau; more and more trees appear in the landscape. Keep left at a fork, following AUSTIS, soon coming into a wooded region of granites and passing a shady fountain on the right (159km 🍴). Take the signposted right turn for SAN MAURO and follow the road through the isolated valley of the Riu Mannu before meeting the SS388. Turn left here: after 10km the church of **San Mauro** (169.5km ✝P14; see panel opposite) rises on the hillside to the left. After your visit to this typical country church enclosed by old pilgrims' shelters, go back along the SS388 and continue ahead to **Ortueri** (176.5km). Here, as in the surrounding villages, the houses are built of reddish trachyte. The road winds down into fertile, partly wooded lowlands with scattered vineyards. Bear left towards BUSACHI/ORISTANO, ignoring the right turn to Neoneli. The countryside is now studded with cork oaks, while there is a splendid view from the plateau down into the Campidano.

Ignore the right turn to Ula Tirso. Almost immediately, you can stop on a bend to the left, to savour the beautiful view of Ula Tirso down in a hollow and the flat lowland beyond. Soon you pass the left turn to Samugeo, followed straight away by another right turn to Ula Tirso. Stay ahead on the SS388 as it curls down to **Busachi** (192km). This picturesque village, too, is built from reddish trachyte.

Continue on the SS388 down from the trachyte plateau to the lowland plain, following signposting for ORISTANO. Gradually the dam wall of the Lago Omodeo comes into view. The enormous massif of Monte Arci rises in the southwest. Ignore a right turn to Ghilarza/Ula Tirso/Paulilatino and then a left turn (Allai/Ruinas). Soon cross a bridge below the dam wall. Monte Arci now rises directly ahead of you in the distance. The road winds its way above the green Tirso Valley. Turn left at the next junction and cross the old arched

SAN MAURO

Surrounded by typical pilgrim shelters (*kumbessias*), the pilgrimage church of San Mauro stands isolated in the Barbagia. As at other remote Sardinian country churches, people came to gather here on certain holidays, which involved large celebrations and livestock markets. The church is believed to have been built after an Inquisition judgment, the exact circumstances of which are not known. Perhaps the Spanish court wanted to counteract the continued existence of heathen cults in the Barbagia; it is believed that the spot occupied by the church today previously harboured a non-Christian temple. On the hillside opposite San Mauro the giant's tomb of Funtana Morta and the Nuraghe Talei are located, the latter one of the few *nuraghi* with a rectangular ground plan. San Mauro was built between 1470 and 1480 on a scale based on the Spanish foot (27.8cm/10.9in). The architect therefore almost certainly came from Cagliari, where the Spanish court resided. He used light pink-coloured trachyte, which looks a little like red sandstone. A large flight of stairs, flanked by lions holding the Aragon coat of arms, leads to the entrance. The façade with its ring of battlements and the side walls protruding at an angle is typical Catalan-Sardinian. It looks theatrical, with its large rosette and Renaissance portal, which underlines the demonstration of power.

For scenic effect and in order to make the interior open up like a stage setting, the vaults increase in height by 50cm/20in between the entrance and the choir, which is hardly noticeable at first. The weight of the stone vaults has forced apart the outer walls, making it necessary to add the ugly supportive walls on the outside. The original altar was replaced during the baroque period by the current marble altar from Piedmont.

---

bridge built from trachyte, entering **Fordongianus** (204.5km ✕🛏).

Turn right just beyond the bridge (yellow signpost: TERME ROMANE). Bear right at the next fork and descend to the river flats, where you will find the Roman baths (🈺). There are good possibilities for a picnic along the shady, tree-lined river bank. Continue downstream to pass under the footbridge, then turn left up the road by the *bagni termali* into the village. passing the Chiesa San Pietro with its beautifully carved trachyte facade on the right (✝), followed by the Casa Aragonese on the left. Meet the main SS388 and turn right to continue. The wide and flat Tirso Valley is on your right; the Altopiano di Abbasanta is seen in the background.

Villanova Truschedu (212km) is a small village with beautiful façades. Monte Arci now rises directly to the left (south), while diagonally to the left the Iglesiente mountains are visible in the distance. The road takes you through the northern Campidano via **Ollastra** and **Simaxis** (222km). Irrigation and drainage channels run through the plain; eucalyptus plantations help drain marshy areas, and Spanish reed lines many watercourses. The SS388 crosses the motorway before leading straight back into **Oristano** (232km).

TOUR 6: LOGUDORO

Alghero • Bosa • Montresta • Padria • Bonorva • Rebeccu • Sant' Andria Priu • Burgos • Bottidda • Bono • Ittireddu • Mores • Ardara • Siligo • Nuraghe Santu Antine • Torralba • Bonnanaro • San Pietro di Sorres • Romana • Monteleone Rocca Doria • Villanova Monteleone • Alghero

304km/188mi; approximately 15 hours (two or three days)
En route: Picnic 15-16; Walk 21; Walk 22 is nearby

Varied landscapes, picturesque towns and villages, fine Romanesque churches, imposing *nuraghi* and mysterious 'fairy houses' are visited on this tour through Sardinia's northwest. This region comprises the Logudoro (from *locus torres*), or medieval kingdom of Torres, with its old capital of Ardara. Great plains, steep-sided table mountains, wide plateaus and isolated volcanic cones alternate in the southern Logudoro. Drawing a parallel between this landscape and another region also shaped by volcanism, La Marmora,

River Temo at Bosa

the great explorer of the island, coined the name 'Sardinian Auvergne' (*Alvernia sarda*).

From **Alghero** (🎣🏨🛏✕🚏⊕) follow the coast road south to **Bosa★** (40.5km 🎣🍴🏨🛏✕🚏). Glowing in warm and mellow hues, the houses of the old town gather closely on the northern bank of the Temo. They are dominated by the ruined but still imposing Castello di Serravalle, in medieval times a stronghold of the Genovese Malaspina family. Most of the old houses are built of reddish trachyte which looks similar to red sandstone but is actually of volcanic origin. From the palm tree-lined esplanade there is a beautiful view out over colourful fishing boats to the opposite bank of the river where you can see old tanneries (*Sas Conzas*). From the south side of the old arched bridge shown opposite, the Via Sant'Antonio leads inland past the 16th-century Catalan Gothic church of Sant'Antonio and the church of San Giorgio to the church of San Pietro Extramuros★ (🎣; see panel overleaf). Built in 1073, this plain building has been little altered and is a fine example of Romanesque style.

The tour continues north on a road that snakes through isolated wooded hills to **Montresta** (57.5km). Ignore a left turn signposted to Villanova Monteleone not far beyond the village and descend over the Riu Piccarolu down in the valley. Stay ahead, soon ignoring a left turn. After a short while you cross the Fiume Temo. The road then climbs through the valley of the Riu Mulinu up to **Padria** (72km 🎣✕). Fork sharp right at the main junction here, on the SS292 signposted for SUNI. Bear left towards Pozzomaggiore at the junction not far beyond Padria. Follow the bypass round Pozzomaggiore (76km), but leave it at the crossroads, taking the signposted right turn for SEMESTENE/BONORVA. This road descends into the valley of the Riu sa Puntigia.

You are surrounded by rolling hills. Ignore a right turn signposted to Bosa/Macomer. Soon you pass the small church of San Nicolo di Trullas (🎣) off to the left in the fields; then go by the village of **Semestene** (87km). Join the motorway to the south (91km), but leave it immediately by turning off left for BONORVA. Head straight through **Bonorva** (92.5km) towards BONO. The road winds its way down into a valley where you take the signposted right turn for SANT' ANDRIA PRIU/REBECCU (95.1km), passing the small Romanesque church of San Larentu on a hill to the right (🎣). Leave the main road on a bend to the left and continue ahead (97.5km; signposted); this lane snakes up to **Rebeccu** (99km).

After visiting this quaint hamlet, descend back to the main road and turn right. Soon take the signposted right turn

SAN PIETRO EXTRAMUROS

The church of San Pietro is located approximately 2km from the old part of Bosa, some distance outside the former city wall (*extra-muros* — 'outside the walls'). Constructed in 1073, this early Romanesque building was the main church of a village at the time (the village was later abandoned when Bosa was established). The church is almost entirely unchanged from the days when it was built. The nave, with its beamed ceiling, impresses through its simplicity. Massive rectangular pillars without bases or capitals are connected by simple arches. Few rays of light reach the dim interior through the small Romanesque windows. The apse and the mighty rectangular bell tower were added between 1110 and 1120. At the beginning of the 13th century, on the threshold of the Gothic era, Cistercian monks redesigned the façade with early Gothic arches and a gable top, showing French influence. The yellow sandstone architrave over the main portal shows (from left to right): Paul (with sword), Emperor Constantine (with sword), Madonna with child and St Peter (with key); St Peter is the saint to whom the church is dedicated.

for DOMUS DE JANAS SANT' ANDRIA PRIU. Shortly after passing the country church of Santa Lucia on the right (✝), you reach **Sant' Andria Priu**★ on your left (104.5km ⛪). Dating back to the late Neolithic period, the site boasts a number of fine cave tombs perforating a trachyte rock face on Monte Donna like honeycombs. In later times, such eerie necropoles were believed to be the homes of fairies (Sardinian *jana*, derived from Diana, the Roman goddess of hunting) — hence their name 'fairies' houses' (see panel opposite).

Return to the main road and turn right. Soon go straight ahead past a left turn to Thiesi and the bottling plant for Santa Lucia mineral water (also on the left; 111km). Winding your way up into a more wooded landscape, you eventually emerge on the Pranu Mannu, a plateau studded with scattered cork oaks, where asphodels create a sea of white flowers in spring. Keep right at a fork (119.5km). Turn right again at the next junction, for FRIDA/BOLOTANA (121km). Ignore a right turn signposted to the Villa Piercy (128.5km) and continue towards NUORO/BOLOTANA. Soon pass a left turn (Foresta Burgos) and continue straight ahead towards ILLORAI. Take the next left turn for ESPORLATU/BURGOS and follow the road down the steep wooded hillside of the Catena del Goceano. Crowned by a ruined castle, the conical mount of Burgos appears ahead of you, with its houses snuggling picturesquely in an adjacent saddle. Ignoring the turn-off for Esporlatu and the signposted right turn to Bottidda/Bono, follow the road as it rises to Burgos. Keep left at a fork where both directions are signposted for the village and climb steeply into **Burgos** (142km ◼✕▢). The castle was built in a strategic position to control the

southern entrance to the Goceano, a fertile basin watered by the Tirso.

Return the same way and turn left to **Bottidda** (145.5km). Turn left again at the crossroads in this village. Affording fine views of the Goceano, the road contours along the hillside to **Bono** (150.5km 🏔️✖️🍴). Turn left towards the town hall at the central junction in Bono, but fork sharp right uphill immediately. The road climbs wooded slopes in deep hairpin bends up to the pass of **Ucc' Aidu** (158km), where Walk 21 begins. Crowned by transmitter masts, the summit of Monte Rasu rises to the left. The road continues through the woodlands of the Catena del Goceano, passing the forestry station at **Sa Puntighedda** (162km 🍴P15). Ignore a left turn to Foresta di Burgos (164km) and continue ahead towards ITTIREDDU. The road leads through the valley of the Riu Mannu before running across the basalt plateau of Pranu Mannu. Ignoring a left turn (170km), continue straight ahead towards OZIERI/ITTIREDDU. When you reach the edge of the plateau, a sweeping view to the volcanic Alvernia Sarda opens up ahead.

Continue straight on

DOMUS DE JANAS

Cave tombs (in Sardinian *domus de janas* — fairies' houses) are very common on the island. In the late Neolithic period many Mediterranean cultures built cave tombs to bury their dead, but the most elaborate examples are found on Sardinia, where the practice is linked with Ozieri culture (3400-2700 BC). At this level of cultural development people lived in caves as well as huts clustered in small villages; they cultivated vegetables and grain, farmed animals, caught fish, and created elaborate ceramics and stone vessels.

Initially cave tombs were simple and undecorated, but in later periods many types of chamber tombs developed, right up to elaborate necropolises resembling houses hewn out of the rock, in which the deceased were meant to feel thoroughly at home. Sometimes the cave ceiling has an imitation saddle roof with 'beams' hewn out of the rock, and imitation wooden doorframes. In very elaborate tombs the main room is supported by a pillar. Commonly the chambers are decorated with reliefs and murals which show abstract bulls' horns – an indication of the cult surrounding the bull which was common in the entire Mediterranean. There are also magical false doors without a real opening, which indicate a belief in another life and a division between the realm of the living and the realm of the dead. It is rarely possible to assign precise dates to the caves, because they continued to be used into historical times. Where cave tombs were hewn into acid trachyte rock, skeletons and metal objects would in any case have decomposed. Today the *domus de janas* are mainly used by shepherds as shelter in bad weather, as animal pens, or for storing fodder.

Photograph: Domus de Janas at Puttu Codinu, where there are nine cave tombs. Note the drain groove in the rock passage round the entrance.

past several turn-offs as you approach Ittireddu, the village seen ahead on the hill, to the left of a volcanic cinder cone. Turn left at a crossroads shortly before Ittireddu (177.5km), towards PONT'EZZU/PARTULESI/SAN GIACOMO. This lane runs through a small valley before bending to the right (179km).*

The main tour continues on the lane, passing the small country church of San Giacomo (179.5km 🐢). Soon the cobbled drive to the Domus de Janas Partulesi forks off left (180km). Go through **Ittireddu** (181.5km ✖) and leave the village to the north past more cave tombs (signposted). Meet a T-junction and turn left on the SS128bis, soon crossing the Riu Mannu and the railway. Keep left when you reach a junction, then ignore a left turn and continue to **Mores** (190.5km 🐢), where the parish church has an impressive 19th-century high classical steeple. Go straight through Mores towards SASSARI, then turn right for ARDARA. The road skirts the prominent table mountain of Monte Santo; some volcanic cones can be seen in the background.

Pass a fork on your left which you will be taking on your way back and continue to **Ardara** (201.5km). Nowadays an unimportant village, it was the capital of the small kingdom of Torres in the Middle Ages. Go straight through and turn right at the end of the village, to reach the church of Santa Maria del Regno (🐢); this so-called 'black cathedral' testifies to the importance of Ardara in times gone by.

Return the same way, then take the fork passed earlier which is now on your right; it is signposted to SILIGO and skirts to the right of Monte Santo. You pass the Terme di Mesu Mundu/Chiesa Santa Maria di Bubalis (7-9C; 210km 🐢) on the right and immediately cross the motorway. Soon meet the bend of a wider road and continue ahead (left) to **Siligo** (213km), a well-kept and flower-filled village. One almost gets the impression the locals are concerned about their image, recollecting the harsh truth of Gavino Ledda's famous autobiography *Padre Padrone*.

The next village en route is **Bessude** (216.5km). Continue to a road junction on the outskirts of Thiesi (220.5km), where you turn left. This road bypasses Thiesi and meets a T-junction where you turn left again. Soon go straight ahead past a right turn to Cheremule, following signposting for the CARLO FELICE. Ignore a left turn for Torralba and drive under

*Here you could take a short walk to a Roman bridge by following the field track to the left (signposted PONTE ROMANO). Ignore the first turn on your right (the drive to a farm), but keep right at the next fork. Turn right again at a T-junction. Go straight ahead on a minor track down to the river where the main track swings right through a green iron gate towards a house. You will come upon two surviving arches of a Roman bridge on the river bank.

SAN PIETRO DI SORRES

the motorway. Soon you come to the **Nuraghe Santu Antine★** on the right (228km 🏛; bar). Continue ahead for a short way, before turning left at the railway station. Turn left again at the next road junction. This lane passes the church of N S de Cabu Abbas on the left (⛪), goes over the motorway and meets a T-junction where you turn right to **Torralba** (235km).

Continue straight ahead to **Bonnanaro** (238km). Turning left for CENTRO/BORUTTA, you go through Bonnanaro and then **Borutta** (240.5km). Take the signposted left turn when the road curves right shortly after leaving Borutta. Almost immediately, keep left at a fork, to reach **San Pietro di Sorres★** (242km ⛪).

Return to the main road and turn left. Meet the road to Thiesi again and turn right, going back to the entrance of the village. Turn left here, then turn right at the junction that follows immediately (signposted for ITTIRI/ALGHERO; 246km). Follow this road for some distance before taking the left turn to ROMANA, ignoring the road straight ahead to Alghero. You are now surrounded by wooded hills. Turn right for ROMANA at a junction then, at a T-junction on the outskirts of Romana, turn left, following signposting for VILLANOVA MONTELEONE as you go through **Romana** (263.5km). Meet the SS292 not far beyond the village and turn right towards VILLANOVA MONTELEONE.

Just before reaching the Temo Reservoir, take the right turn (267.5km) and climb in steep hairpins to **Monteleone Rocca**

SAN PIETRO DI SORRES

In the second half of the 12th century, when Pisa flourished economically and culturally, Pisan aristocratic families also settled on Sardinia and commissioned numerous churches built in the late Romanesque style, now commonly called 'Pisan churches'. The Pisan style combined late classical imagery with Moorish influences, which arose out of trading contacts with the Arab world. Typical features include walls striped in two colours, multicoloured encrustations and a lack of figurative imagery. Arcades and miniature galleries divide the walls in a display of ornamental playfulness.

San Pietro is the church of a Benedictine monastery and one of the most important Pisan churches on Sardinia. It was built between 1170 and 1190, on older foundations. Characteristic of its style is the interplay of white limestone and black trachyte stripes. The façade is divided into three rows of blind arcades, the arches of which enclose encrusted windows and rhombi, as in classical antiquity. The interior features a nave and two aisles dominated by the above-mentioned black and white interplay. The vaults, built entirely from black volcanic rock, give the church a quite severe feeling.

ALGHERO

With its historic centre Alghero (literally 'algae town') is one of the most beautiful towns on Sardinia. It was founded in 1102 by the Genoese Doria family, but fell to Aragon in 1353. In the following year, the native population was expelled, and the town entirely populated by Catalans. In the centuries of Catalan rule over Sardinia, Alghero was extended into a mighty fortress, which protected against aggressors from the sea, and also provided a bastion against the rest of the island.

Tourism in Alghero began in the beginning of the 19th century, when the kings of Savoy erected a summer residence at the town, the Villa Las Tronas, which is an exclusive hotel today. The lively old town, with its narrow lanes, tall houses, arches, squares and promenades is surrounded by a wall with mighty towers which is well preserved where it faces the sea.

The magic of Alghero unfolds after sunset, when the evening promenade, the *passeggiata,* begins. In the glow of the street lights, the small lanes lined by tall houses soon fill with people. Young and old stroll through town, chat and joke, *bambini* jump around regardless of the late hour … and old men sit in front of the bars, drinking their *acquavite* and watching the activities.

House and beach at

Doria (268.5km ◼*P*16). This small community nestles like an eyrie on a precipitous limestone buttress, with a big quarry gaping on its flanks. The defiant castle for which the village was named dates from the 13th century, when it was founded by the noble Genovese Doria family. Monteleone Rocca Doria was besieged by Aragonese troops for three years, between 1433 and 1436; the inhabitants stood firm, but finally had to surrender because of famine. The castle was subsequently destroyed; its ruins are still seen on the edge of the village. Most of the villagers moved to nearby Villanova Monteleone, the 'new town' of Monteleone.

Return downhill and continue on the SS292. The road crosses two arms of the Temo Reservoir. Soon you reach the **Necropoli preistorica di Puttu Codinu** on your right (274.5km 🛈; see panel on page 49). The tour continues through **Villanova Monteleone** (281km ✕🖰). A sweeping view opens up when you leave this country town, spanning the entire northwest of Sardinia, as the road descends in deep hairpin bends back to **Alghero** (304km).

❀ Walking ───────

Over the last few years, walking on Sardinia has become quite popular. An increasing number of locals and visitors alike are beginning to explore the varied countryside on foot. This book covers some of the best walking on the island. For quick orientation, the fold-out touring map shows the general location of all the walks. *Do* follow the instructions closely and beware of attempting to walk cross-country — deep gorges and dense brushwood can make such a route either impassable or very hazardous.

Guided walks are conducted by some co-operatives, in the Supramonte for example by the Cooperativa ENIS, Località Monte Maccione, I-08025 Oliena, tel. 0784 288363. The WWF (World Wide Fund for Nature) Sardegna also organises guided walks occasionally. For further information contact WWF, via S. Sonnino 205, I-09127 Cagliari, tel. 070 670308.

W aymarking, maps

Most walks in this book use distinct footpaths, trails and tracks that are all easily followed, although there is also the odd bit of cross-country walking. Very few of the routes are **waymarked**, and there is very little signposting — so you will have to rely on the descriptions and maps in this book. Some routes are cairned; experienced walkers will help maintain these cairns by keeping them 'topped up'.

The **maps** printed with the walks are based on the official Italian topographical maps and have been annotated to show new roads, walking routes, and other information which should be helpful. Should you wish to 'have a go' on your own, you might like to purchase some of these maps. The Italian national survey, Carta d'Italia, covers Sardinia in both 1:25,000 and 1:50,000 scale. The 1:50,000 series was published in the 1990s but is still incomplete. As it is difficult to obtain these maps on Sardinia itself, if you want to buy them before you travel, contact your local specialist map supplier.

W hat to take

Equip yourself properly for each walk, bearing in mind the distance and the height at which you will be walking. It can be quite cool high up in the mountains —

easy to forget, when you are based in a hotel down on the coast. Don't forget to take **raingear** (especially in spring), just for the odd rainy day. Waterproof clothing that 'breathes' (such as Goretex) is best, since it reduces sweating. It is also essential that you wear **sturdy walking boots**, with good grip and ankle support. Some walking routes are on loose soil or gravel, where you could easily lose your footing. A **telescopic walking stick** (or, better still, one for each hand!) will be a great help on rough or steep terrain. They will increase your agility, ease the strain on your knees considerably and let you 'work' with the upper part of your body as well.

Take enough **food** and **water** with you on your walks, as well as emergency rations of high nutritional value, like chocolate, nuts and dried fruit. I would advise you *against* drinking any spring water, but the many proper fountains, clearly labelled *acqua potabile*, are safe (you'll see the locals taking the water in plastic containers). Take at least 1.5l of water with you on any walk over two hours.

Sufficient **sun protection** is also important, especially from May to September. The intensity of the sun can be very high, even if there is some cloud, so *do* take suncream (SPF 12 upwards), a sunhat with wide brim and UV-protective sunglasses.

Below is the minimum recommended equipment for each walk (additional items are listed in the walk introduction as necessary):

walking boots (broken-in)	light cardigan	compass
	sunhat	torch
waterproof jacket (Goretex or similar)	sunglasses	whistle
	suncream	first-aid kit
telescopic walking stick	rain gear	picnic
	plastic ground sheet	water

Walkers' checklist

For your own safety, please remember:

■ **At any time a walk may become unsafe**. If the route is not as described in this book, and your way ahead is not secure, or if mist closes in on a mountain walk, do not attempt to go on.

■ **Never walk alone in remote areas**. If you are going to tackle a difficult walk, you should tell a responsible person (eg someone in your hotel) *exactly* where you are going and at what time you plan to be back.

■ **Do not overestimate your energy**.

■ **Be properly equipped** (see notes above).

■ Please bear in mind that **twilight** is much shorter in these southern latitudes than in northern Europe. Night falls quite suddenly on Sardinia.

- For one reason or another, a **walk may take much longer than expected**; take this into consideration.
- A **torch, whistle, compass** and **first-aid kit** weigh little, but could save your life.
- Finally, **do not take any risks** and do not walk cross-country through uncharted terrain or without a map on unknown paths.
- Read the '**Important note**' on page 2 and the **Country code** below, as well as guidelines on grade and equipment for each walk you plan to do.

Country code

Agriculture is the main source of employment for the rural population on Sardinia. Please remember that, although the landscape appears picturesque to us, for most people here life means hard work. People should be respected, as well as their land. Don't take anything from the gardens or fields. You can buy fruit and vegetables cheaply at the local markets or directly from the farmer. These simple guidelines are obvious, but important:

- Help to protect the wildlife.
- Leave gates as you find them.
- Do not frighten animals.
- Walk quietly.
- Don't pick grapes or other fruit.
- Take all your litter away with you.
- Be friendly and polite.

Landscape in the Marmilla

Organisation of the walks

There are walks for all abilities in this book. You might begin by looking at the large fold-out touring map inside the back cover. Here you can see at a glance the overall terrain, the road network, and the orientation of the walking maps. There is at least one photograph for every walk, to give you an idea of the landscape.

Each walk begins with some basic planning information: distance/time, grade, special equipment and how to get there. Pay particular attention to the ascent. A total height gain of more than 500 metres/1600 feet is pretty tough going for the average walker. If the **grade** is beyond your scope, don't despair! There is sometimes a short or alternative version of a walk, and in most cases these are less demanding.

When you are on your walk, you will find that the text begins with an introduction to the overall landscape and then quickly turns to a detailed description of the route itself. **The words *path*, *trail*, *track* and *road* have specific meanings in the walking notes**. *Path* means footpath, not usually wider than 0.6m/2ft. *Trail* is used for old routes, worn by time, for example stone-cobbled trails such as old charcoal burners' routes. These are generally up to 2m/6ft wide. *Track* refers to an unsurfaced vehicle track, whether used by 4-wheel drives, farm vehicles or even motor cars. *Roads* are surfaced, with asphalt or concrete.

The **time checks** given at certain points always refer to the total walking time from the starting point of the walk, based on an average walking rate of 4km per hour and allowing an extra 15 minutes for each 100m/330ft of ascent. These time checks are not intended to pre-determine your own pace, but are meant to be useful reference points. Please bear in mind that these times include only brief pauses where you might stop to recover breath or orientate yourself. A walk might easily take you twice as long if you allow ample time for protracted breaks — picnicking, photography and nature-watching.

Below is a key to the **symbols** on the walking maps:

secondary road	●→ spring, fountain, etc	☧† church.shrine
tertiary road	P picnic suggestion (see pages 14-16)	○ charcoal burners' terrace, limekiln
minor road, street		
unsealed road	☞ best views	▣ watchtower
track	🚌 bus stop	⊞ cemetery
old trail	◆ railway station	⊼ picnic tables
path, steps	⊟ car parking	⋔ transmitter.pylon
2→ main walk	■□ building.enclosure	▥ map continuation
2→ alternative walk	■ castle, fortress	⌂☼ rock formation.mill
	✕⌒ quarry, mine.cave	⋜ electricity sub-station

1 CAPRERA

Distance/time: 12.3 km/7.6mi; 3h45min

Grade: moderate. Clear paths and gravel tracks; total height gain of 300m/985ft.

Equipment: see pages 53-54

How to get there and return: 🚗 car ferry to La Maddalena and then by 🚌 (4.5km). There are ferry sailings approximately every 20 minutes from Palau (where Car tour 1 begins) to La Maddalena. There are two ferry companies (Saremar and Enermar); tickets are sold in the harbour kiosk/cafeteria, where a timetable is also displayed. The passage takes about 15 minutes. Leave La Maddalena by heading west along the promenade, and keep right along the main road, passing the military barracks. Cross a narrow causeway that takes you over to the neighbouring island of Caprera. From the end of the causeway, continue for about 350m/yds before parking your car by the roadside — where a footpath forks off right into the *macchia* and an asphalt road turns diagonally left on the opposite side.

Note: The island of Caprera is popular with the locals on weekends. They tend to *drive* on the roads followed in this walk, so it's a good idea to do the walk on a working day, when the island is quiet and peaceful.

Caprera ('Goat Island') is largely covered by light wood-land and *macchia*. Most parts of the island were declared a nature reserve in 1980, to prevent them being developed. This walk initially threads through high coastal *macchia*. A short and gentle climb onto the island's central ridge follows, from where there are magnificent views over the surrounding Archipelago della Maddalena. A gun emplacement dating back to World War II is seen on Poggio Rasu, and a short detour takes you up the island's highest peak. Finally, you stroll to the former retirement home and country estate of Guiseppe Garibaldi, Italy's most popular 19th-century freedom fighter.

Start out at the small CAR PARK by the side of the road. Follow the footpath to the right (south), into the *macchia*. Among the many plants flourishing in this area are tree spurge, asphodels, rock roses, mastic trees, myrtle, gorse and acacias. Keep straight ahead on the main path past any short paths branching off right, down to the coast. Continue ahead when you reach a track junction below a WHITE BUILDING (seen up on a hill to the left; **15min**). The track soon passes a GROVE OF UMBRELLA PINES. Turn right at the fork just beyond a small BUILDING. There is a small cove to your right in the Golfo di Stagnali, fringed by a coarse-sand beach of weathered granite — as are all beaches on the Gallurese coastline.

Continue straight ahead on the main track until you join an asphalt road which you follow to the right. Bear left at the fork soon encountered (the 'Museo geomineralo-gico' is signposted to the right here). A short time later you reach a major road junction. Here you take the first road on your left, which begins to climb gradually. Looking back, there is a sweeping view over the Archipelago della Maddalena with its many islands and indented coastlines. Beyond the strait of Bonifacio in the northwest,

View to La Maddalena from the ferry crossing

the neighbouring island of Corsica is seen in the distance.

You approach a gun emplacement dating back to World War I, spread out to the right, on the western flanks of Poggio Rasu. This peak is easily recognised by the transmitter mast on its shoulder. When the road bends to the left (**1h10min**), a right turn would take you into the barracks, nestling with camouflaged rooftops covered by greenery on a flat patch of hillside. If, however, you carry straight on along the track from this bend in the road, you can walk on an embankment to the gun emplacement on **Poggio Rasu** ('Bare Hill'; **1h15min**). Some rusty iron girders testify to the bridge that once led across the moat, but since this bridge has become dilapidated, you have to go down to the right, into the moat, and climb back up on the other side. Built from local granite into the rocky outcrops, the well-camouflaged gun emplacement, seen against the magnificent backdrop of the archipelago, is a powerful evocation of recent history.

Return to the bend in the road first reached at the 1h10min-point and turn right to continue on the road. It keeps climbing for a short distance (looking back there is another good view of the military site) before it levels out and begins to descend. Meet a T-junction with another road and turn right. Pass a CONCRETE BUILDING on the right and an old derelict FOUNTAIN on the left, on a bend (**1h45min**).

Keep straight ahead on the road for another six minutes or so, until you reach a lay-by on your left. Continue ahead

for about 50m/yds, then fork sharp right uphill on a side-track, to make a short detour. Climbing the side-track, you reach a DILAPIDATED HOUSE. Take the steps that begin here, up to the highest peak on Caprera, **Monte Teialone** (212m/695ft; **2h15min**). The peak is crowned by an lookout post from World War II. The main peak is fenced-in and officially closed because the forestry department runs a weather station up there.

Return to the road and turn right to continue. The road runs north in an almost dead-straight line. Eventually you pass a DERELICT HOUSE on the left (**2h45min**). Not far beyond it, follow the road as it bends left, ignoring the track straight ahead. The asphalt runs out immediately and you reach a track junction where you turn down to the left (the track straight ahead leads up to a gun emplacement on Monte Arbuticci). Pass two turns on your right in quick succession and continue straight ahead on the main track.

At a junction, fork left up a track (initially concreted), passing TWO ENCLOSED BUILDINGS (*ZONA MILITARE*) on the right immediately. The track crosses under a POWER LINE and ascends to a RESERVOIR (**3h15min**). Cross the dam wall and follow the ascending path from the end of the wall. Eventually, the path flattens out and continues on a level contour (now somewhat overgrown, but still fairly distinct). After a short while you come to a CAR PARK. Follow the granite-cobbled drive to the right, past some weirdly-shaped granite rocks punctuated by *tafoni* (see panel page 19), to the **Casa Garibaldi** (**3h25min**).

Just before reaching the buildings, a short concrete drive on the left descends to a small TERRACE and private car park. From the terrace continue downhill through the under-growth on a path that runs below the fenced-in estate. Unfortunately, this area is often full of litter. Soon the path descends between rocks. When you reach a SMALL HOUSE, skirt to the right of it, along its fenced-in garden, then join a road and follow it past houses. Keep left on the main road at a wide junction. Ignore two turns on your right, both leading to the Club Med, and regain the small CAR PARK where you set out (**3h45min**).

2 MONTE LIMBARA

Distance/time: 16.3km/10.1mi; 5h

Grade: moderate to strenuous. Good tracks throughout, with no special requirements: ascents totalling 450m/1480ft.

Equipment: see pages 53-54; there are some springs en route where you can fill up your water bottles.

How to get there and return: 🚗 only by car; 12km from Tempio Pausania. From the town centre, drive east past the railway station and cross the tracks. Leave the main road after about 100m/yds, on a bend to the left, by forking right on the SS392 towards Oschiri. Follow this road for about 6km, then take the signposted left turn to the Località Vallicciola (this is the 139km-point in Car tour 1). The mountain road climbs in steep hairpin bends to Vallicciola, a signposted forestry station at 1000m/3300ft. An asphalt road (Viale dei Martiri Cendio) turns right here and leads past some forestry houses; there is a small picnic area with a fountain in the wood opposite and ample parking by the roadside.

Shorter walks: With the aid of the map, there are various possibilities for short cuts. Two options are outlined below.

1 **Omitting the summit climb** (10km/6.2mi; 2h50min; moderate, with a total height gain of 180m/590ft). If the weather isn't very promising, you can omit the summit climb by turning sharp right (instead of bearing left) at the 1h20min-point. After 200m/yds you meet the asphalt road. Turn right for a few paces, then turn left immediately on another track (where the road bends left). Now follow the main walk from the 3h30min-point.

2 **Short-cut via the helipad** (14.2km/8.8mi; 4h25min; moderate, with a total height gain of 410m/1350ft). If you feel tired towards the end of the walk you can take a short-cut by turning right (instead of left) at the junction encountered at the 4h10min-point. This will take you past a helipad for the fire brigade, from where the continuing road is surfaced. It takes you straight back to Vallicciola; keep right at the junction near the first forestry houses.

O nly a stone's throw away from the lively Costa Smeralda, the serrated granite ridges of the Gallura in the northeast attract walkers because they are remote. Monte Limbara is a massive upheaval rising near Tempio, its weird rock formations sculpted over millennia by wind and weather. Culminating at Punta sa Berritta (1362m/

On the slopes of Monte Limbara

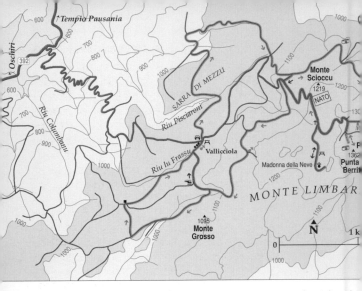

4467ft), it is the third-highest mountain range on the island. A whole network of fine forestry tracks criss-crosses the wooded flanks of the mountain. From the summit, sweeping views encompass most of northern Sardinia as well as the neighbouring island of Corsica, good visibility provided. An area covering some 20,000ha (50,000 acres) of Monte Limbara has been declared a nature reserve and is under protection. There is abundant wildlife, including wild boar, foxes, Sardinian wild cats *(Felis libyca sarda)*, woodpigeons, swift, Corsican deer *(Cervus elephanus corsicanus)* and moufflons.

Start out on the small plateau of **Vallicciola** by turning left from the access road (just opposite the point where the Viale dei Martiri Cendio turns right) on a gravel track that leads into lush woodland. There is a wealth of different trees, including sweet chestnuts, pines, tree heather and wild pear trees. After a short while you cross a gurgling brook called **Riu Pisciaroni**. Then the track rises across the **Sarra di Mezzu** and leads past a minor track branching off sharp left. Soon, when you reach a fork in front of a small stone wall (**40min**), turn right uphill.

Go straight over a crossing of tracks (**1h10min**). About ten minutes later you join a track running obliquely east/west (**1h20min**): continue to the left — almost straight ahead. *(Shorter walk 1 turns sharp right here.)* A short while later you pass **Monte Scioccu** (1219m/3998ft) on the right, a ridge with weirdly-shaped rock formations. Soon a splendid view opens up out over the Val di Rèna ('Valley of Sand'), with the rocky ridge of Monte Bianco (1150m/3772ft) rising beyond it. This ridge is characterised by a

series of enormous bell-shaped domes. Hidden in this area is the Conca di li Banditi ('Cave of the Bandits'), a typical granite cave created by erosion *(tafoni;* see panel page 19). There is little doubt that such caves not only served as a good shelter for shepherds, but also as a hideout for outlaws in the past.

Continue straight ahead uphill past a left turn that leads down into the wooded valley. When the track swings right and almost doubles back on itself, you have reached the most easterly point of your walk. Soon you pass the **Sorgente Bandera** on the left. Keep climbing, before passing close by a number of TRANSMITTER MASTS. Meet the access road and turn left uphill for about 200m/yds, to the summit region of **Monte Limbara**, culminating at **Punta sa Berritta** ('Cap Peak'; 1362m/4467ft; **3h**). It is very rewarding to explore this area with its bizarre rock formations at leisure, enjoying sweeping views in all directions. Looking northwards, there is a sweeping view across wooded valleys out over the upper reaches of the Fiume Liscia; on a clear day the north coast and Corsica are visible. Mountainous country, partly rocky and partly covered by *macchia*, stretches to the southeast — impressive for both its vastness and isolation. A long drawn-out depression reaching from Olbia to Oschiri via Monti is seen in the south; this is the natural boundary between the Gallura and the Nuorese.

To continue the walk, go back down the access road past the track you came along. After ten minutes ignore the left turn to the Chiesa Madonna della Neve. (There is, however, a shady PICNIC AREA along this track, with stone tables, benches and a spring, if you want to take a break.) As you follow the road downhill there are good views of Monte Limbara's wooded slopes. Soon you pass the entrance to a fenced-in NATO area on the right and continue to descend. Ignore a track joining from the right some ten minutes later. *(Shorter walk 1 joins here.)*

Leave the road straight away, on a bend to the left, and fork left on another track (**3h30min**). Once again you become immersed in luxuriant deciduous woodland with sweet chestnut trees. Bear left when you reach a fork in the track, soon passing a CONCRETE WATER TANK on the left. **Monte Grosso** ('Big Mountain'; 1095m/3592ft) rises on the left, its rocks weathered by wind and water. Meet another junction and turn sharp left (**4h10min**). *(But turn right for Shorter walk 2.)* You begin to descend gently; there is a small RESERVOIR in a hollow down to the left which is fed by the Riu Contra Manna. Bear right at the fork near the reservoir, now climbing steeply.

Soon keep to the main track as it swings right, ignoring a minor track off left. Turn right when you join a crossing track (**4h40min**), where you can see a small dilapidated STONE HOUSE beyond it in the meadow. This main track leads you straight back through the shallow valley of the **Riu lu Frassu** ('Ash River') to **Vallicciola** (**5h**).

3 MACCIONE • SCALA 'E PRADU • SOS OSTIS • PUNTA SOS NIDOS • MACCIONE

Distance/time: 7.5km/4.7mi; 3h45min

Grade: moderate to strenuous. This 'out and back' walk follows clear tracks and paths up to the Scala 'e Pradu, from where you continue cross-country to the summit. Depending on the route chosen, the final section involves a little bit of scrambling over rock. Turn back at the Scala 'e Pradu if there is low cloud and mist; the pathless section would be very dangerous. Continuous climb of 650m/2130ft on the outward leg and a corresponding descent on the return.

Equipment: see pages 53-54

How to get there and return: 🚗 by car from Oliena (starting point for Car tour 2). Follow the main street through Oliena towards Orgosolo. Ignore a right turn to Nuoro on the outskirts of Oliena and continue ahead for another 100m/yds, when the road bends right. Fork sharp left here (there is a signpost to MACCIONE/ALBERGO COOP. ENIS). This road skirts the edge of Oliena and then forks: keep right on the concrete road and begin to climb steeply in hairpin bends through woodland. The concrete surface ends at Maccione; the lodge run by the Cooperativa ENIS is on your left, where there is also a car park.

Short walk: Maccione — Scala 'e Pradu — Maccione (5km/3.1mi; 2h35min; technically easy, but a continuous climb of 515m/1690ft on the outward leg and a corresponding descent on the return). Follow the main walk until you reach the end of the track (turning area) at the Scala 'e Pradu (1h35min), then return the same way.

Hidden in the dense holm oak forest that covers the steep flanks of the Supramonte high above Oliena, there is a rustic lodge with a bar/restaurant run by the Cooperativa ENIS. From here you follow tracks and paths over wooded hillsides all the way up to lofty crags. Quite unexpectedly, a sweeping view unravels, out over a stark limestone plateau that is only visited by shepherds and keen trekkers. This desolate scenery looks almost unreal. The final (pathless) section of the walk takes you to the Punta sos Nidos. Rising on the northern flanks of the massif, this summit affords a splendid view of the surroundings.

Start out on the GRAVEL TRACK that continues to the right at the end of the concrete road at **Maccione**, ignoring the left turn to the Cooperativa ENIS. Almost immediately you pass a green ELECTRICITY SUB-STATION. Then pass a promontory on the right with a cross on top, a good vantage point. Leave the gravel track a few minutes later and fork left up a path that climbs through the holm oak forest. The ground has been churned up in places by semi-wild boar searching for acorns. When the path rejoins the track (**30min**), continue uphill in zigzags, initially on cobbles. Keep left on the main track at a fork, following a yellow signpost to MONTE CORRASI (**45min**); the right-hand fork is signposted 'Daddana'.

The track leads past a minor right turn and some shepherds' HUTS AND PENS on the left (**55min**). The oak forest thins out as you quickly gain height; gnarled old trees that have survived clear-cutting are scattered on the stony slopes. Over the treetops you already have glimpses of the lofty limestone crags which you are about to reach. There is a splendid view of the Cedrino Valley, with Oliena seen far below on the foothills; it looks like a toy village from up

Track at the Scala 'e Pradu

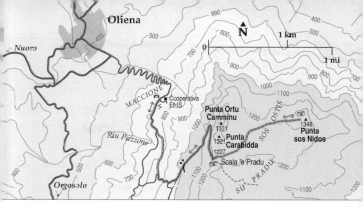

here. The mass of houses comprising Nuoro straddles a ridge in the distance like an unsightly mirage.

Steeply climbing the last section of the **Scala 'e Pradu** ('Steps of the Meadow') below lofty crags, the track ends at a TURNING AREA on the cliff-top (**1h35min**). *(The short walk turns back here.)* Quite unexpectedly, an impressive view of the desolate, almost surrealistic limestone plateau of Su Pradu unfolds. A small path is seen snaking down into the depression, leading to some shepherds' dwellings lost in this stark landscape. The plateau is surrounded by the highest peaks of the Supramonte — Monte Corrasi on the right (at 1463m/4800ft the highest summit of the entire massif), Punta Carabidda on the left and your goal, Punta sos Nidos, diagonally to the left (due northeast).

From the turning area, continue by walking cross-country (visibility permitting!) straight towards Punta sos Nidos, keeping more or less on a level contour. En route you have to cross a slight depression called **Sos Ostis**. The rough limestone outcropping is badly eroded by karstification (see panel page 32), with countless grooves and sharp-edged rocks slowing down your progress.

Finally you reach the cairn-marked summit of **Punta sos Nidos** ('Nests' Peak'; 1348m/4421ft; **2h15min**). From up here you enjoy a bird's-eye view of the fertile Cedrino Valley with its reservoir and the basalt plain of Gollei. Monte Tuttavista dominates the coastal plain on the Golfo di Orosei. If you look to the east, the enormous valleys of Oddoene and Lanaittu are deeply carved into the Supramonte. The houses of Dorgali are spread out below Monte Bardia, a rounded peak crowned by a transmitter.

After you have taken a well-deserved break, retrace your steps via the TURNING AREA (**2h45min**) to **Maccione** (**3h 45min**). It is very relaxing to sit on the terrace of the lodge run by the Cooperativa ENIS and end your day here, enjoying the fresh air while listening to the cheerful birdsong.

4 PONTE SA BARVA • SCALA DE SURTANA • SA CURTIGIA DE TISCALI • SCALA DE SURTANA • PONTE SA BARVA

Distance/time: 10km/6.2mi; 4h30min

Grade: moderate to strenuous, with ascents totalling 440m/1440ft. On the last section of the climb to Monte Tiscali you have to clamber up over rocks on all fours. The rocky sections are very slippery in wet weather.

Equipment: see pages 53-54

How to get there and return: 🚗 only by car. Follow the SS125 from Dorgali to the turn-off 1km south of the tunnel leading to Cala Gonone (Car tour 2 at the 279km-point). Watch your kilometre readings from this turn-off: descending this winding road, you meet a T-junction (1km) and turn left downhill. Follow this road round to the right at the point where a road continues ahead (2.4km). Then follow the road round to the right again where a gravel road continues ahead (4.6km). Go straight ahead past a track branching off right through an iron gate, and you will come to a small country church with surrounding *kumbessias* (6.1km; if you have time, this small bucolic complex merits a brief visit). Follow the road as it bends right,

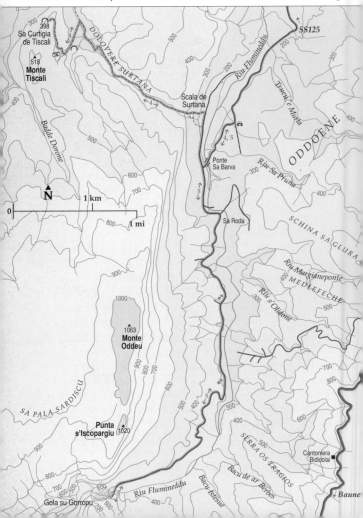

ignoring a minor road off to the left (8.3km). The road eventually crosses a small bridge and bends right just beyond it. The asphalt ends here (at time of writing); a track turns left that has been asphalted for just the first few metres (10.2km). This junction is the best place for parking an ordinary car. The walk begins on the gravel track to the right.

Note: A fee (5€) is charged by the ranger when you visit the Tiscali cavern.

Flanked by steep wooded hillsides, the isolated Lanaittu Valley dissects the northern Supramonte. Monte Tiscali rises at the head of the valley, a bold ridge that you will climb from the neighbouring Flumineddu Valley on the far side of the Scala de Surtana. Two secluded prehistoric settlements are hidden in the huge limestone cavern on the ridge — an utterly stunning and unexpected sight in this desolate wilderness. Built under the protection of overhanging rock,

Sa Curtigia de Tiscali

the crumbling stone walls of these small dwellings date back to the dim and distant past, when Nuragic people settled in this wilderness.

Start out at the FORK WHERE THE SURFACED ROAD ENDS by following the gravel track to the right. It soon leads down to the **Ponte Sa Barva (10min)**, a wooden footbridge that spans the **Riu Flumineddu**. Lined by alders and oleanders, the river rushes through a lush valley. Cross the bridge, go up the opposite embankment for a few paces, and turn right at the junction. Now follow this track straight ahead through high *macchia* for less than ten minutes, before turning left at a wooden sign towards TISCALI. *(Note: this is the second turn on your left. The first one is passed a few minutes earlier; it could also be taken but is more difficult.)* You are now following a well-trodden path through the bushes. It soon begins to climb over limestone rocks. From time to time, waymarks hewn into the rock help to confirm you are on the right route. The path climbs the steep flank of the Valle di Oddoene via the **Scala de Surtana**.

Ignore the path straight ahead when you reach a fork; instead, clamber up right over rocks very briefly (**45min**). Soon you follow an earthen path again, ignoring a sharp turn on your left (this is the alternative route up from the valley). The old shepherds' path ascends more comfortably in a wooded saddle called **Surtana**. Eventually the path levels out in the undergrowth and begins to lead downhill. The path branches in an open area with ancient gnarled Phoenician junipers, where another wooden sign announces TISCALI (**1h30min**).

Ignore the path that descends to the right down into the Lanaittu Valley, but follow the path to the left uphill. Soon you can see a ROCK FACE WITH A CAVE OPENING in the wall just ahead of you. The views now improve as the path climbs in a few zigzags. Flanked by steep wooded hillsides, the Lanaittu Valley extends to the north. An *azienda* (farm) with olive groves is spread out on the wide valley floor.

As you continue to climb, weathered limestone rock with sharp-edged grooves is seen by the side of the path. You pass some beautiful specimens of Phoenician junipers with gnarled trunks and roots. Eventually the earthen path gives way to craggy rocks. Watch carefully for the painted RED ARROWS that frequently waymark the ascent. Rising steeply, you will now have to clamber on all fours in places. Take note of the route — perhaps leaving some markers —, as the waymarkers are not so easily seen in the way down.

All of a sudden, the collapsed limestone cavern of **Sa Curtigia de Tiscali** opens up in the craggy ridge; its entrance is clearly marked. Step down into the cavern. Alerted by the tinkling of a bell, the ranger will hurry over to greet you **(2h15min)**. When you have paid the admission fee, you can either ask the ranger to show you around or you could take a self-guided tour. If you choose the latter, follow the roped-off path in an anti-clockwise circle through the cavern. At its lowest point, under the high overhanging rock faces, the crumbling stone walls of TWO SETTLEMENTS can be seen in the rubble. Judging by its imposing location, this sheltered place must have been virtually impregnable. The middle of the cavern is covered by masses of debris from the collapsed roof. Some giant trees thrive here; it's an idyllic and protected spot — just as one wants it to be.

When you have left the cavern, you could make a short detour to the left after a few paces (before the descent begins). The path climbs over rocks, affording a beautiful view out over the surrounding mountains. At one place you can look down into the huge collapsed cavern from the cliff-top *(take utmost care on this section!)*.

After a rest in the cool shade of the trees, return the same way to the FORK WHERE THE SURFACED ROAD ENDS **(4h30min)**.

Lanaittu Valley

5 PONTE SA BARVA • VALLE DI ODDOENE • • GOLA SU GORROPU • PONTE SA BARVA

See map pages 68-69
Distance/time: 14km/8.7mi; 4h
Grade: moderate out-and-back walk, with a short, steep descent at the end
Equipment: see pages 53-54
How to get there and return: See Walk 4, page 68

Flanked by steep wooded hillsides and rocky escarpments, the Valle di Oddoene stretches south of Dorgali. Splitting the limestone massif of the Supramonte, the famous Gola su Gorropu is a giant defile in the rock face. With its

rock sheer walls rising over 400m/1300ft, this is one of the largest clefts in Europe. The popular walking route takes you along little-used tracks through the lush Oddoene Valley and below towering cliffs to the entrance of the defile.

Start out at the FORK WHERE THE SURFACED ROAD ENDS by following the gravel track to the right. It soon leads down to the **Ponte Sa Barva (10min)**, a wooden footbridge that spans the **Riu Flumineddu**. Lined by alders and oleanders, the river rushes through a lush valley. Cross the bridge, go up the opposite embankment for a few paces, and turn left at the junction. Now follow this track south through high *macchia* with strawberry trees, tree heather, mastic trees, myrtle, and rock roses *(Cistus)*.

Bear right at a junction reached after ten minutes (the track down to the left leads to the river flats of 'Sa Roda'), and go through a wooden gate almost immediately. Bear left at the next junction (**30min**). Pass a SPRING by the side of the track (**40min**) and ignore a right turn just afterwards. The track eventually runs near the river and you pass another SPRING on the right (**1h10min**) before climbing again.

Eventually you pass two imposing holm oaks by the track (**1h45min**). Ten minutes later, descend rather steeply to the mouth of the **Gola su Gorropu (2h)**. Carefully force your way through the thicket of oleander and occasional fig trees that thrive in the stony river bed, until you reach the entrance to this enormous rocky cleft. You can penetrate a short distance into the ravine, but huge boulders and water-filled rock pools will soon hamper your progress.

Over millions of years, the Flumineddu has carved itself deeper and deeper into the Supramonte. Today this lime-stone massif is strongly eroded. Underground drainage explains why no river is seen in the ravine. However, if you go 'downstream' for about 50m/yds, you will reach a geological boundary between the karstified limestone of the Supramonte and crystalline rocks that crop out in the Valle di Oddoene. Here the Flumineddu comes to the surface between stone slabs and rock pools, to continue its course as a rushing river through the valley.

After a well-earned rest, return the same way to the CAR PARK (**4h**).

Left: entrance to the Gola su Gorropu. You can penetrate a short distance into the ravine, but huge boulders and water-filled rock pools will soon hamper your progress.

6 CALA GONONE • CALETTA FUILI • CALA DI LUNA

See also photograph page 2   **Distance/time**: 10km/6.2mi; 3h

Grade: moderate, with climbs totalling 190m/620ft. Some short sections involve a little bit of scrambling over rocks.

Equipment: see pages 53-54; optional: swimwear; the bar/restaurant Su Neulagi at Cala di Luna is open during the season.

How to get there: 🚗 by car to Cala Gonone (Car tour 2 at the 287.5km-point). Park at the harbour.
To return: ⛴ by boat from Cala di Luna back to Cala Gonone. Regular sailings during the season (from Easter until end of September). Ticket sales and information on sailings at the harbourside kiosk in Cala Gonone. (Ticket office: tel 0784-93305; Main office: tel/fax 0784-93302.

Alternative walk: Caletta Fuili — Cala di Luna — Caletta Fuili (13km/8.1mi; 4h; moderate to strenuous, with ascents totalling 360m/1180ft). Access: 🚗 to/from the car park above Caletta Fuili. If the boat isn't operating, you can begin the walk at Caletta Fuili. Follow the main walk to Cala di Luna and return the same way.

The crystal-clear colours of the sea, glaring-white lime-stone cliffs, and lush vegetation in all shades of green contrast wonderfully on the Golfo di Orosei. First you follow a road lined by oleanders, then an old shepherds' path which threads through coastal *macchia* to Cala di Luna. Backed by towering limestone cliffs, this is arguably the most beautiful sandy bay on Sardinia. Set at the mouth of a gorge with an oleander-filled valley floor and a small lagoon, it is the perfect place to relax — knowing you can comfortably take the boat back to Cala Gonone.

Start out at the HARBOUR in **Cala Gonone**. Walk along the beach, then follow the seafront past hotels and restaurants. Leaving the last houses behind, past a car park, continue along the beach. Turn right up a path into the *macchia* when some rocks block your way. Bear left along the hillside when you reach a fence, then climb up to the road and turn left to continue. Lined by beautiful oleanders, the road runs above the magnificent coastline, affording good views of the azure Golfo di Orosei. The road ends at a small CAR PARK above **Caletta Fuili** (**1h**).

Here you look down into the rocky ravine of the **Codula Fuili**, its mouth is fringed by a small sandy cove facing the sea. Mastic trees and splendid oleanders thrive on the gravelly floor, forming an almost impenetrable thicket. From the end of May, the oleanders here will be in full bloom. Descend steps down into the ravine (**1h05min**) and cross it. The path zigzags uphill on the opposite side of the ravine and meets a fork after five minutes: keep right uphill.

The way ahead is waymarked in regular intervals by GREEN ARROWS and other symbols painted on the rocks.

74

Initially you scramble up an outcrop of limestone. The path is well-trodden and runs quite a distance inland, far away from the coastline, crossing rocks and scree through a mixed coastal *macchia* with some high trees. Most common are mastic trees, myrtle, wild olive trees, rock roses and tree spurge. Note, too, the beautiful old Phoenician junipers with their gnarled and twisted trunks.

Eventually the path curves left; this bend is flanked by some STONES on the ground. Keep straight ahead on the main path at a CAIRN some five minutes later, ignoring a path up to the right (marked by red arrows). A short while later an old grassy CHARCOAL BURNING TERRACE is seen on the left. Beyond another CHARCOAL BURNING TERRACE and a hole in the karst rock to the left, continue ahead on the well-trodden path, ignoring the old, overgrown charcoal burners' path that forks off sharply to the right.

Descend into a small valley, where you ignore a left turn; then climb again. Ten minutes later you pass the **Crotta Oddoana (2h 15min)**, a limestone cave in the rock face to

the right. From here you have to scramble down steeply over *breccia* (sedimentary rock composed of angular limestone fragments). When you reach the floor of the **Codula di Oddoana**, keep right on the ascending path, ignoring the left-hand fork down to Cala Oddoana. Some five minutes later, continue straight ahead uphill, ignoring another fork to the left.

From the slopes of **Fruncu Nieddu** ('Black Hill', referring to the dark volcanic rock; **2h35min**) you enjoy a first glimpse of Cala di Luna diagonally below. The path swings to the right, inland. A steep descent over loose stones takes you down to the wide valley floor of the **Codula di Luna** (**2h50min**). Surrounded by a dense thicket of oleander, the

Cala di Luna

river has created a brackish lagoon *(stagno)*, which is very typical at the mouth of many Sardinian rivers. The whitish limestone called *pedra de luna* ('moon stone') is believed to have given the ravine its name.

Turn left (towards the sea) at a STONE PILLAR on the sandy valley floor, then turn right after some 50m/yds at another STONE PILLAR, crossing the thicket of oleanders and alder trees. You come upon another STONE PILLAR in the middle of the valley floor, where poisonous thorn-apples with their prickly capsules thrive abundantly. Go through a wooden gate to reach the BAR/RESTAURANT SU NEULAGI.* A few more paces will take you out to the magnificent sandy beach of **Cala di Luna** (**3h**). Apart from swimming and sun-bathing, you can inspect five CAVES which open at the bottom of the cliffs to the left. The JETTY from where the boat leaves is to the right, at the end of the beach.

*Note: In spring you may not be able to reach the bar/restaurant by heading directly towards the sea because there is too much water blocking your way. In this case you first have to go about 100m/yds to the right (inland), until you are almost level with the two caves that can be seen on the opposite wall. Now cross over to the other bank and follow the gravelly valley floor through scattered stands of oleander towards the sea. Join a path and go through the wooden gate to reach the bar/restaurant.)

CHARCOAL-BURNING TERRACES AND LIMEKILNS

Up to the middle of the 19th century, mixed deciduous forests were common on Sardinia, but with the start of industrialisation clear-felling erased large areas of wood. The timber of the holm oak was used as fuel in the smelting of ores, for railway sleepers, and for the production of paper. By 1910 around one quarter of the total area of Sardinia had become deforested. Charcoal burners were used around that time everywhere in the hills. Their round stone terraces can still be commonly seen today on walks through the mountains.

Charcoal was an important fuel, used in blast furnaces and for the production of lime. In order to increase its combustibility and reduce its weight by 75-80%, the wood was smouldered in kilns. For this process the timber of the holm oak was stacked into cones on the charcoal-burning terraces and then covered with clay. Air could enter the structure from below, through the loose stone foundation, and escape through a central shaft in the kiln. After ten to twelve days the kiln was opened and the charcoal cooled with sand. The yield was generally around 2000 to 3000 kg (2 to 3 tonnes) of charcoal per kiln.

Today it is not unusual to find the remains of limekilns in the vicinity of charcoal-burning terraces. They can be recognised as circular pits in the ground, surrounded by a wall. The limestone stacked in these hollows was covered with stone slabs and soil. In order to heat these limekilns, large quantities of charcoal were needed — approximately ten tonnes in order to extract 100 to 150 tonnes of quicklime in nine to fifteen days. Slaked lime was an important building material, used for mortar and for rendering.

7 GENNA CROCE • CUILE TELEVAI • CODULA DE SA MELA • PLANU CAMPU ODDEU • GENNA CROCE

Distance/time: 15.4km/9.6mi; 4h 25min

Grade: moderate, with ascents totalling 320m/1050ft. The walk follows mostly clear tracks and road; there is also a short cross-country section. Not recommended in low cloud or fog.

Equipment: see pages 53-54

How to get there and return: by 🚗 or 🚌 on the SS125 to the Genna Croce (also spelled Genna Cruxi; Car tour 2 at the 255.5km-point). At this pass a small road branches off to the west (there is a sign indicating 'Comune di Urzulei' among various other places); opposite is a building (Bar/Gelateria

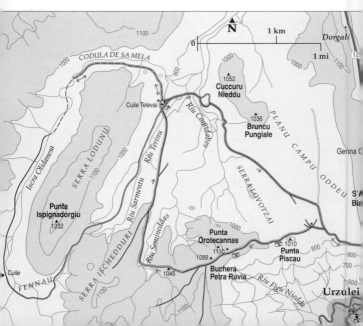

Sa Domu e S'Orku). ARST buses ply this route between Dorgali and Baunei; enquire about times at kiosks or telephone ARST: 0784-32201.

Short walk: Omit the detour into the valley of the Codula de sa Mela (11.8km/7.3mi; 3h15min; moderate, with ascents totalling 240m/790ft). Access and return as above. Follow the main walk but, when you reach the Cuile Televai (2h), turn right on the road, following the notes from the 3h-point.

Photo: escarpment of the Supramonte above Urzulei, on the road where the walk begins and ends

Above the village of Urzulei, a vast limestone plateau stretches at some 1000m/3300ft above sea-level. Overlooked by some rocky ridges, this isolated pastoral landscape with its scattered shepherds' outposts has a stark beauty. The walk follows old trails and the new access road.

Start out at the **Genna Croce** ('Cross Pass'). Follow the small road that branches south off the SS125; it is cut into the rocky escarpment of the Supramonte. The steep slopes are dotted with large holm oaks, while the bright-white crags further up the hillside stand out brilliantly against the blue sky. From the beginning you enjoy a breathtaking view south over the garden valley of Urzulei, with ridge after ridge rising in the distance. There is a bird's-eye view of the village, too, spread out some 400m/1300ft below you. Go through an iron gate and soon reach the edge of the **Planu Campu Oddeu** ('God's Plain'), an isolated plateau on the Supramonte di Urzulei (**30min**). This stark landscape is covered with herbs, asphodels, spurge and low juniper bushes — plants disdained by the livestock, since anything edible is grazed away.

Leave the asphalt road almost immediately after you have reached the plateau, and fork left on the gravel track that runs towards a SMALL HOUSE. Keep to the main track as it swings left past three minor tracks forking off to the right, leaving the house on your right. Gradually gaining height, you approach the **Punta Orotecannas**, where there is a SHEPHERDS' OUTPOST on the hillside to the right (**1h10min**). From here you have another splendid view down into the valley of Urzulei on your left and to your outward route behind you, where the small road at Sa Losula is cut into the rocky escarpment of the Supramonte. Soon cross a small saddle and keep right at the fork, slightly downhill. Keep right again when you reach another fork after 100m/yds.

The path peters out on a SMALL PLAIN IN FRONT OF A ROCK; an animal PEN is somewhat hidden behind bushes on the

left. Continue to walk due west (in the same direction as before, but now pathless), past the rock. Your goal is the track on the opposite hillside. You descend between bushes and trees to cross the **Riu Semi-neddas** (**1h30min**); there are some refreshing rock pools here. Climb the opposite bank for a short distance and, when you meet the contouring track that you spotted from the other side, follow it to the right.

Ten minutes later another track joins sharply from the left; continue straight ahead. The track becomes wider and more stony as it runs in a straight line along the ridge of the **Serra Ischedduri**. You gradually approach the Cuile Televai, a shepherds' outpost with two sheds and a bigger house. Cross the **Riu Terinu** and meet the road opposite the **Cuile**

Televai (**2h**; *the Short walk turns right along this road*). Go towards the house, then skirt the fence above it (below a small house), heading diagonally right. You rise up into woodland with large holm oaks and peonies; hellebores with fine-toothed leaves and greenish flowers thrive here too in the shady undergrowth.

Initially the way is not so obvious, but soon a rough old stone-laid charcoal burners' trail hewn out of the rock takes you into the dry valley of the **Codula de sa Mela** ('Rock-strewn Ravine of the Apple'). The forces of erosion have created this rocky ravine cut deeply into the dolomite. This stark and almost unreal landscape is dotted with splendid specimens of oaks and Phoenician junipers, the scant remains of the former forest. The CHARCOAL BURNING TERRACES seen en route testify to the intensive clearing of trees for the production of charcoal.

The trail contours along the hillside before gradually descending to the gravel-strewn VALLEY FLOOR (**2h30min**). While the outcropping rock consists of dolomite, the rubble in the stream bed comes from the surrounding areas. The colourful pebbles thus resemble a small geological cross-section of the catchment area. Due to underground drainage, however, the river itself only surfaces temporarily, after strong rainfall. Take a break and perhaps find some particularly nice pebbles before retracing your steps to the **Cuile Televai** (**3h**).

From here you follow the road to the left, across the dammed stream, and then uphill. Soon you climb through woodland with more holm oaks. Then the trees begin to thin out and the road crosses the **Planu Campu Oddeu**. You can sometimes avoid the asphalt by following a cows' path beside the road. Bear right at a wide fork, soon regaining the EDGE OF THE PLATEAU (**3h55min**). Retrace your outgoing route along the road, back to the **Genna Croce** (**4h25min**).

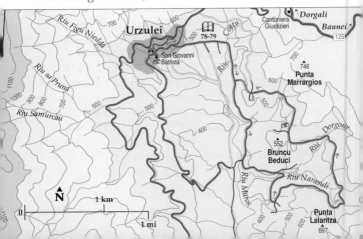

8 URZULEI • RIU COTTU • URZULEI

See map opposite

Distance/time: 9.2km/5.7mi; 2h30m n

Grade: easy, with a total height gain of 280m/920ft.

Equipment: see pages 33-54

How to get there and return: 🚗 by car. Take the turn-off for Urzulei from the SS125 (Car tour 2 at the 252.5km-point). This road winds down the hillside and takes you straight into the village, where you can park in Piazza Fontana (4km from the SS125).

Below the isolated mountain village of Urzulei, a green garden valley stretches southwards. Numerous streams tumble down the surrounding hillsides; they all feed the Riu Cottu. This walk follows comfortable tracks along wooded slopes, with good views of the pleasant valley.

Start out at the church of **San Giovanni Battista**, a plain building dating from the 17th century, in the lower part of **Urzulei**. From its terrace there is a good view to the south over the garden valley of the Riu 'e Gurue ('Brook of the Wood Thistle') which is surrounded by wooded slopes. Step back through Via Parrocchia for a few paces, then follow the cobbled village street (VIA SAN GIOVANNI) to the right. Go straight ahead at the next junction on VIA MANNO, ignoring Via G Deledda down to the right. Bear left on VIA NUORO at the following fork, ignoring Via Ogliastra down to the right. Leave the street when it climbs to the left past house No 8 and descend an asphalt lane to the right.

Leaving the village, you begin to walk down into the valley of the Riu Cottu. Leave the road on a wide bend to the right and continue straight ahead on a track. Keep left at a fork in front of an iron gate. Soon cross the stream bed of the **Riu Cottu (15min)**. The paved track swings southwards and runs along the eastern slopes of the main valley, past gardens, fields and pastures. Cork oaks stand by the side of the track; if their tree trunks glow in rusty red colours their bark has just been stripped off. Keep straight ahead on the main track.

Just before reaching a bridge in the main valley you climb steeply left uphill on a stony eroded track (**45min**). Soon the wooded side-valley of the Riu Narasuli comes into view. The track levels out and begins to descend gradually; bear right at a fork. Cross the **Riu Narasuli (1h05min)** and continue to the left on the main track. It bends to the right straight away and climbs the wooded hillside. Turn left when you reach a junction some five minutes later. This track, easy under foot, initially descends slightly, then winds very slowly uphill and re-crosses the Riu Narasuli and then the **Riu Dorgone (1h30min)**, both on concrete fords. Keep on this track for some time, enjoying the splendid views.

When the track forks on a saddle (**1h40min**), where **Bruncu Beduci** rises on the left, keep right. Urzulei is seen in the valley down below, spread out on the foothills of the limestone escarpment of the Supramonte. Reach a crossing of tracks by a TRANSMITTER (**2h**) and descend diagonally to the right (opposite the iron gate) on a footpath leading into cork oaks. This path is stony in sections; it leads quite steeply downhill before rejoining your outward track (**2h05min**). Turn right to retrace your outward route back to the church of **San Giovanni Battista** in **Urzulei** (**2h30min**).

In the valley of the Riu Cottu

9 CHIESA SAN PIETRO DI GOLGO • SU STERRU • AS PISCINAS • ANNIDAI • CALA GOLORITZE • CHIESA SAN PIETRO DI GOLGO

Distance/time: 10km/6.2mi; 4h

Grade: moderate, with a drawn-out climb of 470m/1540ft on the way back. The walk follows tracks and stony paths.

Equipment: see pages 53-54; the Ristorante Golgo is near the start of the walk.

How to get there and return: 🚗 only by car on the SS125 to Baunei (Car tour 2 at the 232.5km-point). Take kilometre readings from here. *Coming from the south,* fork right up Via San Pietro diagonally opposite the main church in the town centre (just past the town hall; 0km). This street is signposted to GOLGO etc. Meet a wide T-junction and turn sharp right uphill. Turn sharp left at the next road junction (in front of a fountain; 0.8km). This road passes a transmitter and climbs in steep hairpin bends on the flanks of the mountain. Reach the plateau and pass a right turn (2.1km; this short detour would lead you to a terrace with panoramic view). Follow the road across the plateau, ignoring several forks. The asphalt ends shortly after you have passed a right turn signposted 'Piscinas/Voragine/ Goloritze' and a left turn to the Ristorante Golgo; continue ahead on the dirt road. Soon you reach a fork with signposting to the left for the Chiesa San Pietro and ahead to Cala Sisine: continue straight ahead. The dirt road branches again after 300m/yds in front of a stone wall; this time you turn left (sign: CHIESA SAN PIETRO). After just 100m/yds, turn right through a gate in the stone wall, to reach the enclosed church. You can park under the shady old olive trees, which is also a good picnic spot.

This invigorating walk in the Supramonte di Baunei leads through a wild valley down to the Cala Goloritze. Fringed by a beautiful sandy beach that can only be reached on foot or by boat, this secluded cove is ideal for a relaxing break with a dip in the sea. But first of all you visit an isolated pilgrimage church. And there is more to discover — a gaping cavity in the limestone plateau which was caused by erosion and underground drainage. In spring, idyllic pools form between dark basalt rocks not far from here.

Start out at the **Chiesa San Pietro di Golgo**. This small pilgrimage church dating from the end of 18th century is surrounded by the typical Sardinian pilgrims' dwellings (*Cumbessias*) which are reminiscent of a monastic complex. Traditionally used to accommodate the villagers from Baunei when they get together here, these dwellings lie deserted for most of the time and only come to life on feast days, when there is traditional dancing and singing (see panel overleaf). In front of the entrance gate to the enclosed complex (slightly to the left) stands a small menhir, or standing stone, with a slightly weathered human face, bearing witness to a pre-Christian place of worship. It is also interesting to note the arrangement of stones on the ground to the right — perhaps an old tomb. Near the enclosure there are picnic tables under gnarled old olive trees.

Top: the Aguglia, a rock pinnacle above Cala Goloritze, popular with rock climbers; above: the idyllic setting of As Piscinas

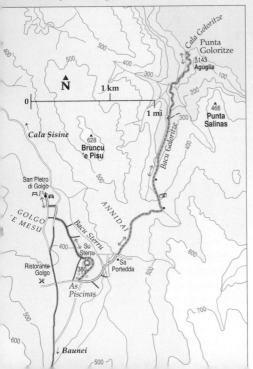

MUSIC

Sardinian music appears archaic and elaborate at the same time; strange harmonies of voices and changes in tempo are typical. Its floating approach and dying away and different kind of tonality appear very alien to our ears.

Some songs are accompanied by *launèddas*, a woodwind instrument with three pipes. A lamenting recitative underlined by the sound of *launèddas*, with its mixture of droning, humming and rattling sounds appears very strange to us. The instrument must have been in use thousands of years ago on Sardinia, as it is depicted on a Nuragic bronze statuette. Learning to play the *launèddas* requires hard training, in which breathing technique is essential: the player breathes through the nose and uses the mouth as an air reservoir in order to create a constant air stream. The *launèddas* make intonation in several voices possible, although this was not yet known in classical antiquity. The large bass pipe *(su tumbu)* serves as an organ point, whereas the two other smaller pipes *(sa mankosa* and *sa mankoseddu)* supply a melodic accompaniment above the bass tone. The greatest challenge of a *launèddas* player is to fill a simple repertoire of melodic phrases *(sas nodas)* with his own variations.

With your back to the entrance gate of the enclosure, go straight back in the direction from where you came by car. After about 100m/yds, go through the GATE in the stone wall and turn left. Turn right at the next fork, ignoring the sign-posted left turn to Cala Sisine, and follow the wide dirt road. Leave it after less than 200m/yds by turning left just past a large cork oak on the left and some 100m/yds before the dirt road gains an asphalt surface. Goats and half-wild pigs roam around freely here. The countryside is dotted with pear trees which produce delicate white blossoms early in April.

Bear right at the next two forks (the second of which is quite faint). Less than ten minutes after leaving the dirt road you reach a junction. Continue straight ahead to the gaping cavity of **Su Sterru** (also called Voragine di Golgo; **15min**) near an information board. For safety reasons, this 270m deep abyss is fenced in. Do *not* climb over the perimeter fence — there is sheer drop down into the abyss, concealed by bushes! (The cross here testifies to a fatal accident.)

Continue ahead on the path with the wooden railing. Hidden between dark basalt rocks, small pools (**As Piscinas**) can soon be seen between the trees and bushes — an idyllic spot in spring. Meet a gravel track and turn left; you immediately come to a wide track junction in an open area, where you turn left again. Stay ahead on this main track past several turns on the right, but bear right on the main track at a Y-fork. This quickly leads you past a fenced-in area on the right, with a house (SU PORTEDDU; **30min**). Leave the track almost immediately, on a bend to the right (by a boulder on the left with the inscription 'GOLORITZE'): climb the clear path here that begins to thread through the *macchia*.

After 20 minutes of climbing you cross the ridge of **Annidai (50min)** and get a first glimpse of the sea. The path continues to wind more or less at an even contour through the *macchia*. Among the many plants are *Phillyrea,* mastic trees, strawberry trees and rock-roses *(Cistus monspeliensis).* Soon rocks come into sight on the right, with a SHEPHERDS' SHELTER built into the side of them. The path gradually begins to descend. A sheer rock face flanks the left-hand side of the **Bacu Goloritze** ravine as you walk down. Pass another SHEPHERDS' SHELTER built into a rock (**1h**). Ancient holm oaks of imposing size dot the landscape, specimens that were spared by the charcoal burners in the 19th century.

Originally well constructed, the old stone-laid charcoal burners' trail is worn by time and crumbling. Follow it as it winds down into the ravine. Further down the **Aguglia** comes into sight. Rising above the Punta Goloritze, this prominent pinnacle is popular with rock climbers. Go through a ROCK ARCH (**1h30min**) and continue to descend. Quite unexpectedly the magnificent cove appears below you. A short but steep descent leads you down to **Cala Goloritze (1h45min)**, a small cove with turquoise water fringed by a glaring-white fine-shingle beach.

When you can tear yourself away from this lovely spot, return the same way to the **Chiesa San Pietro di Golgo (4h)**.

Cala Goloritze

10 BAUNEI • BELVEDERE VISTA PANORAMICA • SCALEDDAS • GENNA INTER MONTES • SANTA MARIA NAVARRESE

Distance/time: 8.9km/5.5mi; 3h

Grade: easy, with an initial climb of 200m/650ft; the rest is all downhill. The walk follows good tracks for most of the way.

Equipment: see pages 53-54

How to get there and return: Since this is a traverse, one leg has to be covered by public bus. Obviously it gives you more flexibility to take the bus first, so you don't have to rush back. 🚗 Drive to Santa Maria Navarrese (Car tour 2 at the 222.5km-point), where there is ample parking. 🚌 ARST buses to Baunei depart from Tortoli Mon-Sat 10.30 and 12.50; these stop about five minutes later at the main junction below the pilgrimage church in Santa Maria Navarrese; journey time to Baunei about 15min. Tickets are sold in the kiosk (Edicola Sa Panada). Alight in the centre of Baunei opposite the main church of San Nicola.

Alternative walk: Baunei — Santa Maria Navarrese — Baunei (18.8km/11.7mi; 6h40min; strenuous, with ascents totalling 880m/2900ft). Access: ARST 🚌 (tel: 0784-32201) or 🚗 to Baunei. Do the whole main walk and return the same way; the return route is mostly uphill.

From Baunei, a hillside village set on the southern flanks of the Supramonte, this traverse threads its way across steep hillsides down to Santa Maria Navarrese, once a place of pilgrimage but now a pleasant resort with a beautiful sandy beach. The houses cluster around the old pilgrimage church that was founded in the 11th century by a daughter of the king of Navarra after she was saved from a shipwreck off the nearby coast. You enjoy beautiful views of the Ogliastra all the way along. Framed by high ridges. this fertile coastal plain opens to the sea near Tortoli.

Start out in the square in front of the parish church of **San Nicola** in **Baunei**. Opposite the church is the town hall. Climb the flight of steps (SCALETTE PIER CAPONI) that ascends on the right-hand side of this large new building. Turn right when you meet an alley, but climb another flight of steps beyond house No 29 almost immediately. Meet another alley and turn right uphill. Then turn left uphill on a street in front of a concrete wall with a green iron railing on top. Fork sharp right in front of house No 93/95, but turn left after a few paces (just beyond the house) into a small side street. It leads past some more houses before reverting to a gravel track climbing quite steeply up the wooded hillside.

When you reach a wide road junction by a FOUNTAIN with the sculpted head of a wild boar (**15min**), go straight ahead to continue the ascent. Pass a TRANSMITTER and follow the road as it winds steeply uphill in hairpin bends. When a rock crowned by an IRON CROSS comes into view on your *right*, the road first bends to the left, then back to the right. Leave

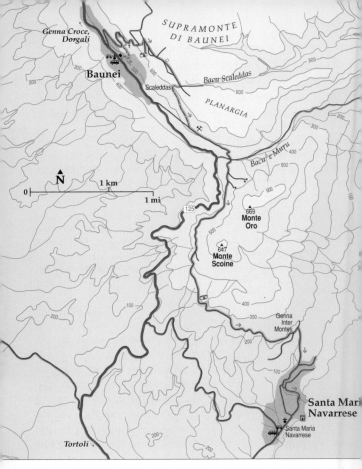

the road in the following left bend (this is the last hairpin before the edge of the plateau) and go straight across a small gravel area, to climb a faint but clear path up the hillside. Soon you reach the plateau of the **Supramonte di Baunei**. Here the path bends slightly to the left and joins a wide gravel-strewn track junction (used as a CAR PARK).

Two tracks lead to the right here and one to the left. Follow the first track to the right through the stone pillars of a gate, to a BELVEDERE (**40min**). From this balcony at the edge of the plateau there is a breathtaking view over the rooftops of Baunei towards the Ogliastra with its colourful tapestry of fields and pastures. Drained by the Riu Pramaera and its tributaries, the fertile lowlands are framed further inland by an amphitheatre of mountains. More mountain villages like Lanusei can be spotted on the distant hillsides. The imposing Gennargentu massif rises in the background.

Return to the wide gravel-strewn track junction and fork sharply to the right. Keep left on the main track at the following Y-fork; the minor track to the right soon rejoins your route. After about 100m/yds, keep ahead, ignoring a left turn. At the next fork, the track branches again, but soon rebraids itself. A circular pit opens in the ground or the left just beside the left-hand branch — an old limekiln.

The track gradually descends into a slight depression where it branches at the lowest point. Here you ignore both the track ahead that climbs to a rock face and another track descending to the left. Instead, turn right and continue (pathless) along the lowest point of the terrain; within minutes a faint path takes you to the edge of the plateau. Here you join an old stony trail and go downhill through a WOODEN GATE (please close the gate behind you). This place is known as **Scaleddas** ('small flight of steps'; **1h**).

Straight away the trail bends to the left and descends the hillside; soon you skirt a WIRE-MESH FENCE. Large rosemary bushes, with marvellous blue flowers in early spring, thrive on these sun-baked slopes. Ignore a couple of forks climbing to left to some shepherds' shelters and continue to descend straight ahead alongside the wire fence. Keep straight ahead past a sharp turn down to the right and continue on an almost level contour above a pine wood, soon passing a quarry on your left. Monte Oro ('Gold Mountain'; 659m/2195ft) is seen ahead of you in the distance while, slightly lower, Monte Scoine rises to the right of it. The track begins to descend more severely, passing more shepherds' outposts and an old quarry now used as a dump for rubble, before leading in a double bend (first to the right, then to the left) down to the road in the valley.

Cross the road in the valley of the **Bacu 'e Muru** (**1h20min**) and climb the asphalt lane on the opposite hillside. Follow the track to the left when the asphalt ends. Soon keep straight ahead on the main track and ignore two forks on the left climbing to more shepherds' outposts. The track contours for the next 15 minutes on the lower slopes of **Monte Oro** and **Monte Scoine**, before you reach a Y-fork (**1h45min**). Bear right through the WOODEN GATE, ignoring the track rising to the left. The track now descends rather steeply in places. A magnificent view opens up, out over terraced fields which have been mostly abandoned. Fringed by long sandy beaches, the entire coastline of the Ogliastra is spread out before you. In the middle, Capo Bellavista juts out into the sea, with the harbour of Arbatax. Purple granite porphyry rock crops out on this headland and on the coastal plain further inland. The Stagno di Tortoli, a lagoon rich in fish but once a breeding-ground of the feared malaria

Descending the Scaleddas

mosquito, extends behind the coast.

Ignore any right turns and stay ahead on the hillside track. Steadily loosing height, you reach the wide end of an asphalt road at the **Genna Inter Montes** (**2h30min**). Cross the car-turning area below this pass and bear right after 25m/yds, to descend the road (VIA MONTES TUNDUS). Continue ahead at the road junction by the first houses of **Santa Maria Navarrese**. Turn left when you reach a major crossroads in the resort, following signposting for 'Centro', and descend alongside a gully. Keep right when you reach a junction and cross the gully on the bridge, ignoring the street down to the marina. Beyond the Hotel Agugliastra, you reach the OLD PILGRIMAGE CHURCH (**3h**); this plain building can only be visited during mass.

Now turn left down to the long sandy beach with its old watchtower. It's a perfect picture-postcard setting, with some purple porphyry rocks rising offshore in the magnificent bay.

MALARIA

Even as far back as classical antiquity, malaria was the bane of Sardinia. Boggy lowlands and coastal lagoons were practically uninhabitable, because the Anopheles mosquitoes — carriers of malaria — had their breeding grounds there. Of course it was not until 1898 that it was recognised that this life-threatening disease was caused by the sting of infected mosquitoes. Before then it was only known that swamps and still waters were dangerous, and people avoided these because of their foul smell (*mala aria* — 'bad air'). At the beginning of the 20th century draining of the swamps was begun, with systematic canalisation and the planting of eucalyptus trees, which grew quickly and therefore absorbed larger quantities of water than other trees. The eucalyptus tree's old name 'fever tree' refers to swamp fever — malaria.

Malaria was not finally stamped out on Sardinia until the 1950s, with the support of the Rockefeller Foundation. Villages and towns were regularly sprayed with pesticides at that time, and the dates of those operations can still be found marked on the walls of some of the older houses (for instance in Bosa).

11 ASCENT OF PUNTA LA MARMORA

Distance/time: 13.5km/8.4mi; 5h return

Grade: moderate to strenuous. Mostly easy climbing of 650m/2130ft overall; only the ascent of Xuxu is quite steep and rocky. The walk follows good trails and paths for the most part. The best months are from mid-May to mid-October; don't tackle this walk in changeable weather or if the visibility is poor.

Equipment: see pages 53-54

How to get there and return: 🚗 by car to the Arcu de Tascuss (Car tour 2 at the 64km-point). Turn left at the crossroads at this pass and follow the road along the hillside until it forks after 4.5km. Bear right uphill and climb in a series of bends (sign: BRUNCU SPINA/PUNTA LA MARMORA). The asphalt road ends after 1.7km at the mountain hut (*rifugio*), at 1505m/4936ft.

At 1834m/6016ft, Punta La Marmora is not only the highest summit in the Gennargentu massif but the highest elevation on Sardinia. Nevertheless, it is not a prominent peak and, were it not for the cross on top, one would hardly be able to locate it on the long summit ridge. The classic ascent to the roof of the island starts out at the *rifugio* and follows the crest of a ridge. The panoramic views from the top, out over the rugged mountain landscape, are breathtaking; on a clear day you can see most of the island. The air is crystal-clear up here, and there is an invigorating feeling of vastness and majesty.

The walk begins at the MOUNTAIN HUT (*rifugio*) that was built some years ago. It stands empty and has sadly fallen into disrepair. Follow the track that climbs above the *rifugio* and swings southeast along the hillside, ignoring a fork

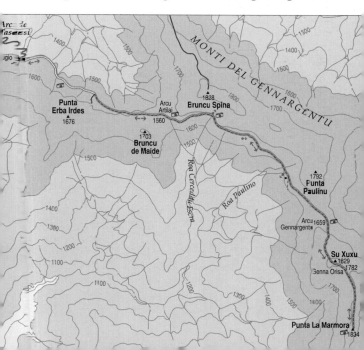

down to the right and a ski run down to the left. There is a sweeping view over treeless pastureland to the north, where you can see the valley of the Riu Aratu cut deeply into the flanks of the mountain, its lower reaches studded with oaks. When the motorable track ends, ignore a faint track leading sharp right uphill and continue straight ahead on the main path (between two wooden signboards), gradually climbing along the hillside towards Bruncu Spina, the mountain diagonally ahead of you to the left. But when you reach the steep flank of Bruncu Spina, follow the main path to the right, up to the **Arcu Artilai (1h)**.

From this saddle, a stupendous view unravels out over wide valleys, to the summit ridge of the Gennargentu massif; screes cover some of the steep hillsides. From left to right you can discern a ridge, then the reddish saddle of Arcu Gennargentu, followed by the rocky peak of Su Xuxu which is crowned by a big cairn. Next comes the main ridge with the Punta La Marmora. From this perspective you have no impression of its height.

Cross the saddle and follow the clear undulating path that contours the hillside. Enjoying splendid views, you first walk on the lower slopes of **Bruncu Spina**. You pass a SPRING on the left, then reach a FENCED-IN AREA with a shady place to rest and another SPRING (**1h25min**); alder trees line the brook that tumbles downhill from here and feeds the Roa Cerceddu Escra further downstream. The path descends slightly and threads its way through rocks, past a second fenced-in area which lies in the upper reaches of the **Roa**

Left: the author on the summit of Punta La Marmora, the highest point on Sardinia; right: the Bruncu Spina, where you'll find two particularly pleasant picnic places.

Paulinu (1h35min), another good picnic spot with shady trees. Nearby you can see the sad ruins of the first MOUNTAIN HUT that was built from granite about a century ago.

Ignoring a minor path down to the right, climb the main path up to the **Arcu Gennargentu (1h55min)**. When you reach this wide saddle , you enjoy a first view of the isolated mountains that extend to the east. From the saddle you start your ascent of Xuxu, the mountain with the reddish rocky peak that rises just ahead. It is best to climb the left-hand (eastern) flank of this mountain. Initially you can follow an obvious path that leads you past a SPRING (enclosed by some piled-up stones) and some scree through the low *garrigue*. Keep right further up the slope to reach the rocky crest, then climb on boulders up to the peak. A big cairn crowns the summit of **Xuxu** ('Escarpment, Rocky Precipice'; **2h30min**).

From Xuxu descend pathless over scree to the **Genna Orisa**. This saddle is also covered by detritus of reddish granite. Follow the easy path that climbs gradually along the main ridge of Gennargentu, leading you directly to **Punta La Marmora (2h55min)**. The summit is crowned by a cross; a broken marble plaque is fixed to a rock. Formerly simply known as Perda Crapias ('Goats' Rock'), the peak was re-named at the end of the 19th century in honour of Sardinia's most famous explorer. If not the world, at least a good part of Sardinia lies at your feet from this highest of the peaks.

When you have soaked up that invigorating 'top of the world' feeling. return the same way to the *rifugio* where the walk began (**5h**).

12 ARITZO • BELVI • STAZIONE DESULO-TONARA • BELVI • CASTAGNETO GERATZIA • ARITZO

Distance/time: 15km/9.3mi; 4h35min

Grade: easy, with ascents totalling 270m/890ft.

Equipment: see pages 53-54

How to get there and return: by ARST 🚌 (tel: 0784-32201) or 🚗 to Aritzo (Car tour 2 at the 87km-point). Part-way through the walk, at Belvi, you take the 🚂 narrow-gauge railway north to the next station, called Stazione di Desulo-Tonara. Enquire about the timetable at Belvi station or get information from the Sardinian Tourist Authority (ESIT, address page 9).

Short walks (both are easy; access/return as above):

1 Circuit without the detour on the railway (10km/6.2mi; 3h20min). Follow the main walk to Belvi and continue straight ahead on the main street past the left turn to the railway station, following the notes from the 2h05min-point.

2 Circuit without the detour to the chestnut grove (10.4km/6.5mi; 3h). Follow the main walk to the track junction not far beyond Aritzo's cemetery (the 2h45min-point) and turn right, following the notes from the 4h20min-point.

Opening hours

Museo etnografico, Aritzo: Sat 16.30-19.30, Sun 10-13 and by appointment (tel 0784-629323; ask for Angela Faba).

Museo Scienze Naturali, Via San Sebastiano, Belvi: only by appointment (tel 0784-629467 or 0784-629397; ask for Benito).

This pleasant circuit begins in the mountain village and traditional summer resort of Aritzo. Sunken tracks lead you past springs and through shady woods down to Belvi, where you can visit the museum of natural history. From Belvi you take the narrow-gauge railway for a short distance, before walking back along the railway track. On your return to Aritzo the route makes a detour to the chestnut grove of Geratzia with its giant trees. At the end of the walk you can visit the interesting museum of folklore (Museo etnografico) in Aritzo.

Start out in the main street of **Aritzo**, diagonally opposite the parish church. Descend a narrow flight of steps (VIA SCALE CARCERI) between houses 50 and 52. Walk under the archway of the OLD PRISON, a building made of undressed slate like most other traditional houses in Aritzo. Turn left down the cobbled alley in front of the prison and continue straight ahead at the following junction on VIA GARIBALDI. Soon a small square comes up on the right, affording a good view of the wooded landscapes to the west of Aritzo.

Continuing ahead on the cobbled alley, you soon leave the last houses of Aritzo behind and descend into a small valley. Here the track swings right past a bubbling FOUNTAIN (**5min**) and climbs to a track junction: bear diagonally left downhill. This paved track leads through coppices of hazel, chestnut and oak trees. Pass another FOUNTAIN with benches on the left, a good place for a short rest (**Funtana di Zi' Arbara; 15min**). A little more than ten minutes later you reach a crossing of tracks where you turn right. (*Ignore* the signpost pointing straight ahead to Monte Texile; this route is not viable at present.) Keep descending straight ahead on this shady and somewhat overgrown sunken track.

At the edge of the forest, near a house down in the valley, you join a gravel track coming from the left: continue straight ahead. Shortly after passing a SAWMILL with some other buildings, you meet the main road in front of a house. Turn right, but fork left on VIA G MARCONI after the bend (signposted to the Chiesa S. Agostino). This road affords a fine view of the wooded valley of the Riu s'Iscara before it leads into Belvi. Pass the parish CHURCH on the left and bear left at the junction beyond it, to come onto the main street in **Belvi (45min)**. Turn left to continue the walk but, before you do so, you may want to have a creamy cappuccino or a *really* strong espresso in one of the bars. (However, if you follow the main street to the right you can make a detour to the MUSEUM OF NATURAL HISTORY. Take the signposted left turn shortly before the end of the village (by the 'Carabinieri', the police station), and bear left on the cobbled street almost immediately. The museum is in the first house on the left.)

Follow the main street past the PETROL STATION in the village centre and take the sharp turn on the left just beyond it (signposted STAZIONE FERROVIARIA). (*For Short walk 1, however, you stay ahead on the main road.*) Go down the road to the left when you reach a small green space (VIA S GIOVANNI BOSCO); it leads straight down to the small RAILWAY STATION, which has been lovingly renovated (**50min**). From here you take the train to the next station, the **Stazione di Desulo-Tonara**, only a few minutes away. This station is quite far away from the villages after which it is named, so it's not surprising that you will see hardly any locals getting on or or off the train!

From the railway station return to Belvi on the small path beside the railway track. Soon you will cross the road, then a high viaduct over the **Riu Bau Desulo (1h05min)**. More than 15 minutes later you cross another viaduct over the **Riu Oecile**. The railway track crosses the road once again before leading back to the station of **Belvi (2h)**.

From the station go back up to the main street (**2h05min**) and turn left. Fork diagonally right uphill after house No 12, on a cobbled street that rises past more houses. Cross a wide asphalt road (Via J F Kennedy) and continue ahead on VIA A DE GASPERI. After a bend to the right, the concreted street reverts to track: continue ahead, passing an iron gate ('No 4') on the right. Fork right after some 20m/yds, up a sunken track, ignoring a level track that continues ahead through a wooden gate.

This sunken track climbs past a house on the right and

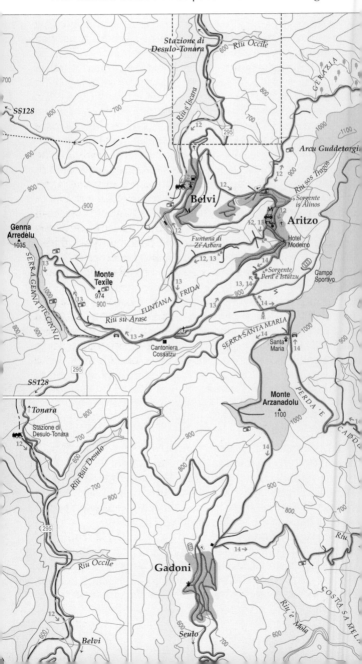

through woodland. Ignore a right turn and bear left at the next fork. Eventually you join an asphalt road and turn left. The road contours briefly on the hillside, before another road joins sharply from the right; descend straight ahead to the Aritzo's CEMETERY (**2h45min**).

Skirt to the right of the cemetery and climb VIA IS ALINOS. A fine view of Aritzo opens up. Continue straight ahead on the concreted track when the road bends right by the first house (*but turn right for Short walk 2.*) Keep following the main track, sections of which are concreted. The views begin to improve; you can see Belvi down in the main valley, while Tonara is spread out on a ridge in the northwest.

Keep left at a Y-fork, to enter the chestnut grove of **Geratzia** with its gnarled old trees. Turn back when you reach a gate some 15 minutes past the Y-fork (**3h35min**); the continuing track soon leaves the grove and peters out. Retrace your steps to the bend in the road by the house (**4h20min**) and turn left to rejoin VIA IS ALINOS. It runs above some houses on the hillside before leading into the small valley of the **Riu sos Tragos**. Opposite is the bubbling **Sorgente is Alinos** (**4h25min**). Watch out you thirsty walkers: the inscription says *si possono prelevare litri 20 di aqua da volta* (you are only allowed to take 20 litres at a time)!

Refresh yourself with this deliciously cool spring water, then follow the paved road downhill. Bear left at a fork on the level paved street (VIA IS ALINOS). (However, if you want to visit the interesting MUSEUM OF FOLKLORE, go straight down the concreted street, cross the main street and follow the

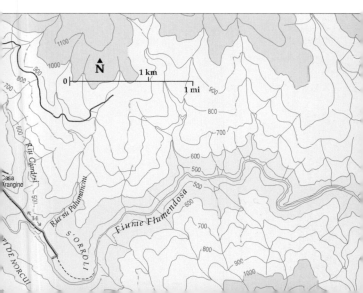

sign next to the petrol station. The museum is housed in the school.)

Keep following the street when it bends left in front of a house, then turn right immediately into Via B Sulis. Keep right at the fork in front of house No 4, an old building with a wooden balcony, and descend Via Arangino to the parish church in **Aritzo** (**4h35min**).

Aritzo

13 ARITZO • MONTE TEXILE • SERRA GENNA PICCINNU • CANTONIERA COSSATZU • ARITZO

See map pages 96-97; see also photograph opposite

Distance/time: 11.6km/7.2mi; 4h05min

Grade: moderate, with climbs totalling 420m/1380ft.

Equipment: see pages 53-54

How to get there and return: by 🚌 or 🚗 to Aritzo (as Walk 12, page 94).

Short walk: Monte Texile circuit (5.2km/3.2mi; 1h55min; easy, with an ascent of only 170m/560ft). Access by 🚗: drive southwest from Aritzo and continue straight ahead past the left turn to Gadoni opposite the Cantoniera Cossatzu. Just 750m (under half a mile) past this junction you can park on a bend to the left, on the verge to the right where the walking trail turns off. Follow the main walk from the 1h10min-point to just after the 3h-point.

This rewarding circuit takes you via shady, sunken tracks from Aritzo to Monte Texile. This imposing limestone buttress (*texile* means stool) affords a magnificent panorama of the Barbagia Belvi and the winding Flumendosa Valley which is cut deeply into the highlands. Then you cross the ridge of the Serra Genna Piccinnu, with sweeping views all along.

Start out in the main street of **Aritzo**, diagonally opposite the parish church. Descend a narrow flight of steps (VIA SCALE CARCERI) between houses 50 and 52. Walk under the archway of the OLD PRISON, a building made of undressed slate like most other traditional houses in Aritzo. Turn left down the cobbled alley in front of the prison and continue straight ahead at the following junction on VIA GARIBALDI. Soon a small square comes up on the right, affording a good view of the wooded landscapes to the west of Aritzo.

Continuing ahead on the cobbled alley, you soon leave the last houses of Aritzo behind and descend into a small valley. Here the track swings right past a bubbling FOUNTAIN (**5min**) and climbs to a junction: bear diagonally left downhill. This paved track leads through coppices with hazel, chestnut, and oak trees. Pass another FOUNTAIN with benches on the left, a good place for a short rest (**Funtana di Zi' Arbara**; **15min**). A little more than ten minutes later you reach a crossing of tracks where you turn left. (*Ignore* the signpost pointing straight ahead to Monte Texile; this route is not viable at present.) Follow this shady sunken track fairly steeply uphill. After less than 15 minutes, keep right at a fork. Initially this track climbs more gently, but then the way steepens again. Turn left when you meet a T-junction, joining an asphalt road straight away (**1h05min**).

Turn right along the road until a track forks off right on a

bend to the left (**1h10min**; *this is where the Short walk begins*). Now follow this track; with the prominent buttress of Monte Texile rising ahead of you to the right. Keep right on the main track when you reach a fork and, almost immediately, continue straight ahead downhill past a right turn. The track (now somewhat overgrown) runs through the valley of the **Riu su Arase** before it begins to climb gradually; there is a good view of Monte Texile to your right. Meet a T-junction and turn right on the contouring track. Then reach another T-junction where the walk will later continue to the left, but turn right for the present. This track leads through a pine grove with picnic tables towards the foot of Monte Texile.

From the end of the track, a path climbs the last section to the foot of the buttress. Turn right; on the western face you can clamber up a gap with some helpful rocky ledges, to reach the flat top of **Monte Texile** (**2h**). The panorama from this natural belvedere is simply breathtaking. There is a sweeping view over the wooded Barbagia Belvi, with the isolated mountain villages of Aritzo, Belvi, Desulo and Tonara spread out on the hillsides. Flanked by some limestone escarpments *(tonneris)*, the winding valley of the Flumendosa is seen in the southeast.

Return through the pine grove to the last T-junction (**2h10min**) and continue straight ahead (originally you came

Shaft of sunlight on Monte Texile during a thunderstorm

from the left) Soon keep left at a fork, then go left again at the next fork. The track rises in a series of bends. The surrounding hillsides are covered with strawberry trees, rock roses, myrtle and tree heather. The views improve as you climb, taking in Monte Texile and the Flumendosa Valley.

The track branches in front of a STONE WALL that runs along the ridge of the **Serra Genna Piccinnu (2h35min)**. Turn left along the stone wall and walk on the crest of the ridge. There is a magnificent view of the Gennargentu massif on the left; soon another splendid vista opens up to the west. After about 10 minutes you walk through a gap in a crossing stone wall. Continue ahead for 40m/yds, then bear left at the lowest point, on a slightly overgrown but distinct trail, and follow it downhill. When you reach a fork, there is a magnificent view of Gadoni and the rocky escarpments that flank the Flumendosa Valley. Bear left and continue to descend until you go through a gate and reach the asphalt road (**3h**).

Turn left along the road. *(The Short walk ends after a few minutes at the place where you left your car.)* After less than 15 minutes you pass a building on the right (**Cantoniera Cossatzu; 3h15min**) and reach a road junction straight away. Climb the hillock ahead of you, up to the SHRINE on top of it, then descend straight down to the lane beyond it. Follow this lane straight ahead, now gradually rising. Some 15 minutes later a concrete track branches off diagonally to the left (from an old bend in the road). Descend this track; it takes you through coppices with chestnuts and oaks. Ignore a left turn and keep downhill on the sunken track.

Pass the **Sorgente Perd'e Istatzu** on the right (**3h55min**) and reach the main street in **Aritzo** just opposite the Hotel Moderno. Turn right to go past the PALAZZO ARANGINO, back to your starting point at the parish CHURCH (**4h05min**).

14 ARITZO • SERRA SANTA MARIA • GADONI • FLUMENDOSA • CASA ARANGINO • PERDA 'E CADDU • SERRA SANTA MARIA • ARITZO

See map pages 96-97; see also photograph page 98
Distance/time: 18.3km/11.4mi; 6h 15min

Grade: strenuous, on account of the length and height gain, with climbs totalling 810m/ 2660ft. Good tracks throughout; easy route-finding.
Equipment: see pages 53-54
How to get there and return: by 🚌 or 🚗 car to Aritzo (as Walk 12, page 94).
Shorter walk: circuit from the chapel of Santa Maria (13.9km/ 8.6mi; 5h10min; moderate, with ascents totalling 630m/2070ft). Access only by 🚗 car: leave Aritzo

to the southwest and take a sharp left turn at the road junction opposite the Cantoniera Cossatzu, following signposting for the CAMPO SPORTIVO (*don't* take the road to Gadoni!). This lane rises gradually and passes a transformer station. After the transformer station, take a sharp right turn. This road crosses the ridge of the Serra Santa Maria; 500m beyond the saddle you reach the chapel of Santa Maria on the right, where you can park. Now follow the notes for the main walk from the 1h-point to the 5h35min-point.
Photograph: the Casa Arangino

T his splendid circuit takes you from Aritzo via the outskirts of Gadoni into the unspoilt Flumendosa Valley. Winding tortuously through the wooded highlands, the Flumendosa is the second-longest river on the island. One could spend hours in this quiet valley, enjoying its solitude and peace; the river banks are cloaked in lush vegetation. On your way back you climb steep slopes studded with cork oaks before you return to Aritzo.

Start out at the parish CHURCH of **Aritzo**. Follow the main street south past the PALAZZO ARANGINO. Fork left up a con-creted alley (VIA MARGINICOLA) opposite the Hotel Moderno, and climb this sunken way past several houses. Beyond the **Sorgente Perd'e Istatzu (15min)**, a fountain on the left, continue ahead up the shady sunken track. It rises through chestnut coppices, before joining an old bend in the road. Bear left to join the new road, cut deeply into the hillside. Find the continuation of the path on the far side and follow it uphill alongside a stone wall. Meet a crossing track by a PYLON and turn left along the ridge of the **Serra Santa Maria**. When the track joins an asphalt road, turn right along it.

Soon the road sweeps to the right; here you can follow a track running parallel with the road. A few minutes later you reach the chapel of **Santa Maria** on the right (**1h**). Turn right on the track in front of the chapel and go through an IRON GATE. Keep straight ahead on the main track, ignoring a minor track that forks right almost immediately. This pleasant forestry track contours through aromatic pines and other trees. In spring, the high, yellow-blooming spikes of giant fennel *(Ferula communis)* brighten the sides of the track.

Eventually you cross an open fire-break and another track, running parallel with each other down the hillside: follow the main track round a left bend. You are contouring along a wooded hillside cloaked with holm oaks, strawberry trees, tree heather and rock roses; *robinias* (false acacias) line the side of the track. There are sweeping views to the right out over mountainous country, with the rooftops of Gadoni further downhill. In the distance you can make out the winding Flumendosa Valley, although the river itself is not visible from up here.

Then the track bends to the right and begins to descend rather steeply; it runs parallel with a fence and then a stone wall. Further down you go through another GATE. Continue straight downhill on the concrete road, ignoring tracks that join on both sides. Two minutes later you reach the outskirts of **Gadoni** (2h), by a BUILDERS' MERCHANT on the right. Leave the road just opposite this fenced-in site, and fork left on a gravel track.

Two minutes later the track forks in front of an IRON GATE. Bear left uphill on the main track, ignoring the minor concreted track down to the right. From now on the walk is quite straightforward: stay ahead on the main track and go past any (gated) forks on either side leading into gardens and coppices. The track runs through the side-valley of the **Riu 'e Mola** (2h15min) before it rises slightly and crosses a small saddle. Then the track begins to wind steadily downhill, with good views to the southeast over wooded hills rising on both sides of the Flumendosa Valley. If you look to the east, a long section of the valley is visible, with Perda 'e Liana rising in the distance — a prominent limestone buttress like Aritzo's Monte Texile. Keep right, downhill, on the main track at a fork reached five minutes after crossing the small saddle.

The track leads through a lush side-valley where you can smell fragrant mint (**2h45min**). Soon you cross another side-valley where you can hear a burbling brook. Then the track rises briefly through shady woodland before it joins another track that descends from the left. *(This is your way back after you have visited the river.)* Continue ahead downhill and cross the **Riu Gierdesi** (3h10min), then the **Riu su Palumancau**. Later the track runs straight through the flood-plain of the river; this area is called **S'Orroli** ('Downy Oak'). Bear right in front of a fenced-in area with a RED IRON GATE, and find your own private picnic place on the banks of the **Fiume Flumendosa (3h25min)**.

Retrace your steps to the track junction where you came from the left (**3h55min**) and bear right uphill. Soon the CASA ARANGINO is glimpsed on the right. Used by shepherds today, this dilapidated house once belonged to the eponymous family of wealthy landowners. A few minutes later, ignore a sharp right turn. The steep hillsides you are climbing are studded with cork oaks; if their bark has just been stripped off their tree trunks glow in rusty red colours. Keep on the main track as it rises steeply in hairpin bends and ignore any minor tracks leading off the bends.

Eventually the gradient eases. Hemmed by stone walls, the track rises more gently on the ridge of the **Perda 'e Caddu**, before it joins an asphalt road (**5h**). Turn left and follow the road uphill. Pass the chapel of **Santa Maria** on the left (**5h35min**) before retracing your steps back to **Aritzo** (**6h15min**).

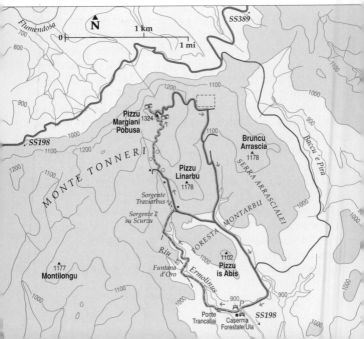

15 THROUGH THE FORESTA DEMANIALE MONTARBU TO MONTE TONNERI

See map opposite

Distance/time: 8.4km/5.2mi; 3h

Grade: moderate, with a total height gain of 480m/1570ft. Some of the trails have been badly churned up by wild boar.

Equipment: see pages 53-54

How to get there and return: 🚗 only by car. *If you come from the east coast,* go through Lanusei on the SS198 (0km) and take kilometre readings from there. Shortly beyond the town, when the road bends to the left (4.3km), take the signposted right turn for Villagrande Strisaili/Nuoro. Ignore the right turn to Atzara. Soon turn left over a small bridge (9.6km) and cross the narrow-gauge railway. The road winds its way above the Flumendosa Reservoir. Keep straight ahead, ignoring the signposted right turn to Gennargentu (19.7km), the left turn to Perda Liana (22.9km) and a gravel road that turns off to the right (36.1km). Take the signposted left turn for MONTARBU 11KM (41.9km). *Otherwise,* follow Car tour 2 and take the right turn at the 149km-point for MONTARBU 11KM. *Whichever way you approach,* you now have to drive 10.5km on a road (mostly gravel) to the Foresta Demaniale Montarbu/Monte Tonneri. After 2.7km on this road, the asphalt ends. Soon you go through the iron gate of a game enclosure; please close it behind you! After another 3km you pass a right turn that leads to a station on the narrow-gauge railway line. The gravel road ends at the forestry station (Caserma Forestale Ula/Mario Falchi). Park your car by the last house, opposite which the gravel track bends to the right through a green and white iron gate.

The state forest of Montarbu is situated miles from anywhere in the wild highlands of the Barbagia Seulo. Its beautiful mixed woodlands cover the limestone plateau of Monte Tonneri. The rocky northern escarpment of this mountain drops precipitously to the deeply-etched Flumen- dosa Valley. In recent years these woods were thinned out and many trees were pruned, to support the growth of a healthy high forest. The walk initially follows the shady valley of the Riu Ermolinus, before climbing through oak woods to Pizzu Margiani Pobusa, at 1324m/4343ft the highest peak in this area. From up here there is a stupendous panoramic view over the wild highlands of eastern Sardinia.

Start out at the FORESTRY STATION. Go between the big house on the left and the picnic area up on the right, to join a trail (SENTIERO ERMOLINUS) that bends to the right imme- diately and runs along the hillside into a shady valley. Cross the **Riu Ermolinus** ('Millstream') on a wooden footbridge (PONTE TRANCALLAI) and continue upstream in the valley, following the course of the brook. Wooden signs along this nature trail give the botanical as well as Italian and Sardinian names for various bushes and trees. Ignore a trail joining sharply from the left. Soon bear right at a fork. The trail continues to follow the Riu Ermolinus and crosses it several

Looking north over the Flumendosa Valley to the Gennargentu massif

times. Deposits of calcium carbonate, forming sinter terraces, are seen in the stream bed. At one place you can also observe that the stream drains away to continue underground before it reappears a short distance downstream — a typical phenomenon of limestone regions.

When the trees thin out you reach a flat and more open area (**50min**). Turn right at a T-junction and cross a brook that is fed by the **Sorgente su Scurzu** (the trail coming from the Funtana d'Oro joins from the left). Follow the trail for another five minutes, until it curves to the right across a stream bed (maybe dry in summer). Ignore a sharp turn on your left to the Sorgente Traviarbus immediately beyond the crossing (this path is rather faint), but take a track that forks left after 25m/yds; it may be signposted to PIZZU MARGIANI POBUSA.

The track begins to rise more steeply through the trees. Watch out as soon as the track flattens out and begins to descend slightly: after some 75m/yds of level walking, just past an old CHARCOAL BURNING TERRACE up on the right, fork right uphill on a path (**1h20min**). This turn-off is marked by a CAIRN and comes up some 75m/yds before the jeep track swings left through a dried-out stream bed where there is a CORRUGATED IRON SHED. After a short while more old charcoal burning terraces are glimpsed — first down on the left, then up on the right. Eventually the path becomes less obvious, but cairns and red waymarks on the rocks clearly mark the ascent. The views begin to improve and, looking back (to the southeast), mountainous country unfolds.

Scramble up the last section over bedrock and scree to reach the summit, which is crowned by a transmitter and a fire-watch post. At 1324m/4343ft, **Pizzu Margiani Pobusa**

One of the rocky escarpments of Monte Tonneri

('Fox Hoopoe Peak'; **1h50min**) is the highest peak on Monte Tonneri, so it's not surprising that you enjoy a truly magnificent panorama from up here. There is an even better view if you follow the path for about 100m/yds to the northwest, where there is a small rise at the edge of the plateau — *but beware of the sheer drop.* Below the rocky northern escarpment of Monte Tonneri is the deeply-indented Flumendosa Valley, with the Gennargentu massif rising beyond it in the background. If you look to the northeast, you can see the prominent buttress of Perda 'e Liana, the big brother of Aritzo's Monte Texile. The Barbagia Seulo stretches out to the south, a stark landscape with rocky escarpments *(tonneris)* reminiscent of the 'Wild West'.

Follow the stony jeep track that begins at the fire-watch post and zigzags northeast downhill towards Perda 'e Liana. (The photograph above left was taken on this track.) When you reach a FENCED-IN FLAT GRASSY AREA (**2h05min**), turn right along the wire-mesh fence. The track bends to the right at the far corner (GATE) of the fenced-in area. Leave the fenced-in area behind, to resume your descent. About five minutes later, keep following the main track downhill to the right, past a faint fork. After another five minutes, continue straight ahead past a sharp turn on your left. Eventually the track bends to the left. Soon you follow the track round a sharp bend to the right, ignoring a minor track that joins from the left. You are now walking parallel with a WIRE-MESH FENCE on the left. Keep straight ahead downhill on the main track, ignoring any turns left or right, until you are back at the FORESTRY STATION (**3h**).

16 GIARA DI GESTURI

Distance/time: 9.4km/5.8mi; 2h45min

Grade: easy, almost level walking. However, route-finding is not easy on the second part of the walk (from the *pinnetta*). This section should only be tackled by experienced walkers with a good sense of orientation; otherwise see the Alternative walk suggestion. Don't do *any* part of the walk in low cloud or mist. After strong rainfall large areas of the plateau may be flooded; all the tracks will be muddy and quite impassable. Don't leave the described route: one can easily get lost on this featureless plateau.

Equipment: see pages 53-54; also compass if available

How to get there and return: 🚌 only by car to Tuili (Car tour 3 at the 134km-point). Turn right when you enter the village, following signposting for the ALTOPIANO DELLA GIARA. At the next fork you have a choice: either bear right or continue straight on (there are signposts pointing in both directions). Cross a bridge at the edge of the village and keep right at the fork just beyond it. Follow this tarred lane up to the car park at the edge of the Giara di Gesturi (5.5km from the bridge at Tuili).

Alternative walk: From the car park via the Paùli Maiori to the *pinnetta* and back (6km/3.7mi; 2h10min; easy). Access as above, no compass necessary. Follow the main walk as far as the *pinnetta* (1h40min), then retrace your steps back to the car park.

The northern part of the Marmilla is dominated by the Giara di Gesturi, a huge basalt plateau of volcanic origin that drops steeply away to the surrounding hills. The plateau is studded with cork oaks and rock roses *(Cistus monspeliensis)*. A number of shallow lakes *(paùli*; derived from the Latin *palus,* 'swamp') appear on the rather impermeable basalt layer during the rainy season, with yellow and white flowering buttercups *(Ranunculus aquatilis)* growing in the water. Reminiscent of African savannahs, a blue sky spans this seemingly endless plateau. Small half-wild horses are often encountered on the shores of the *paùlis*. They roam about freely on the Giara and nourish themselves on the lush aquatic plants. Aeons ago, two flat volcanoes spilled out lava over the entire plateau; this walk takes you to one of them, Monte Zeparedda.

Start out from the CAR PARK by going straight ahead on the main track through the GATE, ignoring the information hut (VIGILANZA SA GIARA) on the right. (But, if the ranger is there, you might like to talk to him.) The track forks straight away: bear left, following a sign: CHIESETTA SANTA LUISA/ PANORAMA 150 M (later you will be taking the right-hand fork). A short detour takes you to the **Chiesetta Santa Luisa**. This chapel stands at the edge of the Giara. From here there is a splendid view to the south over the rolling hills of the Marmilla ('Breast'; see photograph page 55). The focal point of this landscape is the eponymous conical mound near Las Plassas. Its peak is crowned by a ruined castle, once an important stronghold of the judges of Arborea. Scattered around this bucolic countryside are friendly farming communities like Tuili and Barumini.

Return to the fork and turn left through the gate (please close it behind you), to continue on the main track It runs past a high METAL MAST close to the edge of the plateau. You reach a track junction near a FARM which is enclosed by a stone wall: keep right. The track leads through the gap in a stone wall. Then it runs between two parallel stone walls about 30m/yds apart. After about 80m/yds the track leads through a GATE in the wall to the right. Turn left beyond the gap and follow the track parallel with the wall.

The track passes a SQUARE DRYSTONE ENCLOSURE on the left. (Here a detour of just 80m/yds to the left would take you to the Nuraghe Tutturuddu.) Continue ahead on the main track, ignoring a right turn. Soon ignore another right turn; you will be taking it on your way back. You reach a T-junction in front of a large CIRCULAR DRYSTONE PEN (**30min**). A right turn would take you straight to the shore of the Paùli Maiori, but first turn left and follow the walled track.

Almost immediately, the **Paùli Piccìa** ('Small Marsh') comes into sight ahead of you to the right; this lake is normally dried-up in summer. The track is still flanked by a stone wall on the left, while the lake extends on the right. You are walking on a slightly raised track that has been roughly cobbled with stones, a *highway* in the truest sense of the word. The track swings right, then left almost imme-

diately, at the end of the lake, and leads back to the stone wall. As you approach an iron gate at the edge of the plateau, fork left just before it. Go through the grass along the edge of the Giara to reach a small spur. Covered by earth and greenery, an inconspicuous heap of stones is all that remains of the **Nuraghe Nuridda**, a tower once rising proudly on the edge of the plateau (**45min**).

Return the same way to the circular drystone pen and continue ahead to the shore of the **Pàuli Maiori**, where the track peters out. Turn right along the shore of the lake and walk past a small stand of cork oaks, to reach an open wet area. Now turn northeast, away from the lake, and follow the small watercourse that feeds the lake for about 250m/yds upstream until you reach the **Mitza Salamessi** (**1h15min**). This picturesque fountain is reminiscent of holy wells from the Nuragic era; the spring water flows into three cattle troughs.

Retrace your steps to the turn mentioned before (just before the 30min-point); it will now be on your left. You reach it about five minutes after having turned left again at the circular drystone pen. Soon you come upon the ROUND HUT shown opposite (called *pinnetta* in Sardinian), where the track peters out; nearby are some OLD PENS with stone walls and vaulted roofs (**1h40min**).

The walk continues on the main trail which runs to the right (east) of the hut at a distance of about 50m/yds. *(If you opt for the Alternative walk, retrace you steps from here back to the car park.)* This trail is not easy to locate, as it is overgrown at the outset, but it becomes clear within a minute and leads past a menhir-like STANDING STONE. Be sure to follow the main route — an earthen trail that is viable in a jeep, and ignore any of the paths branching off into the bushes. A few minutes after leaving the *pinnetta* you reach a fork: bear right on the main trail, and pass between two cork oaks after just 25m/yds. If you look diagonally to the right across the plateau which is covered with rock roses, you can see a slight wooded rise — this is Monte Zeparedda, where you are heading. When you reach another fork, this time bear left on the main trail (*ignore* the path to the right, even though it leads towards Monte Zeparedda). Follow the main trail round to the right at the next fork.

Turn right when you reach the track junction opposite a GATE in a stone wall (**1h55min**), but fork left after just 50m/yds. This track leads into the cork oaks and runs close to a stone wall on the left. Take the first turn on your right, away from the wall. Soon you cross another stone wall and

On the Giara di Gesturi: approaching the Pauli Maiori (right,, and the pinnetta (left). These round huts, with conical roofs covered in foliage, were traditionally used by shepherds as a shelter when they were tending their sheep for days and weeks far from home. Their construction is reminiscent of the huts from the times of the Nuragic people.

continue straight ahead. Leave the track where it bends to the left (just in front of a cork oak tree with two trunks, with a stone wall some 50m/yds behind it): fork right on a path that climbs the basalt rocks. Surrounded by oak trees, this idyllic spot is like a big rock garden. At the highest point, a metal IGM plaque on a rock marks the TOP OF **Monte Zeparedda** (**2h05min**).

Go south for some 50m/yds, until you reach a small stone pen in the shadow of some oak trees. Turn right (west) towards the iron mast that can now be seen in the distance, and head slightly to the right of it; this pathless section leads slightly downhill through shrubs. About a minute later, you reach a flat area. Some stone enclosures with a ruin and a SMALL STONE BUILDING, with its original vaulted roof still intact, appear on the left (**2h15min**). This building is now used as a pen. It is reminiscent of similar stone constructions in Ireland, like the Gallarus Oratory.

With your back to the stone building, turn right for some 50m/yds, until you meet a track. Follow this to the left. Continue ahead when another track joins sharply from the right after two minutes. Turn left at a crossing of tracks, and follow the wide track to the southwest. You can still see some remains of the old stone cobbles. A stone wall on the right begins to run parallel with the track. Reach a fork where you follow the wide main track round to the left, ignoring the track straight ahead into enclosures. Soon you pass the fenced-in **Giardino botanico della Giara**, followed by two cattle troughs on the right. Follow the main track round a bend to the right, then walk round a fenced-in area on the right and go through a wooden gate (please close it behind you), to regain the CAR PARK (**2h45min**).

17 PUNTA PINNETTA • CAPO SPARTIVENTO • (MONTE SA GUARDIA MANNA) • TORRE DI CHIA • PUNTA PINNETTA

Distance/time: 16km/9.9mi; 4h40min

Grade: easy. Hardly any ascents except for the optional climb of Monte Sa Guardia Manna (176m/577ft).

Equipment: see pages 53-54; optional: bathing things

How to get there and return: 🚗 by car from Pula. Take the SS195 towards Teulada. Not far beyond the pass of Arcu de Generuxi, take the signposted left turn for CHIA at the 43km road marker. You soon reach the main crossroads in Chia, with the Bar Mongittu on the left (refreshments, telephone; supermarket in season). Continue for another 5.5km on the coast road, until a small holiday camp with an entrance gate is seen on the left at Punta Pinnetta (not far beyond a small col). This is the 61km-point in Car tour 4. At the entrance gate there is a signpost, 'Perdalongu'. Park by the side of the road, but do not block the entrance.

Short walk: Since this is an out-and-back walk, you can make it as long or short as you like, by turning back at any point.

The Costa del Sud, extending between Capo Spartivento and Capo Teulada, comprises the southernmost stretch of the Sardinian coastline — less than 200 kilometres away from Africa. Due to strict building regulations, the Costa del Sud is mostly unspoilt and boasts some glorious sandy beaches. Since Capo Teulada is a military area closed to the public, this walk takes you to Capo Spartivento, the 'Cape where the wind parts'.

Start out at the entrance to the holiday camp, by the signpost 'PERDALONGU' near **Punta Pinnetta**. Descend the path to the right of the gate, alongside the fence and eucalyptus trees. Continue ahead on the track when the fence ends, to reach **Cala Antonarieddu**. Swing left round this pretty cove and climb the path above the coast, enjoying a magnificent view of the seascape at the southernmost point

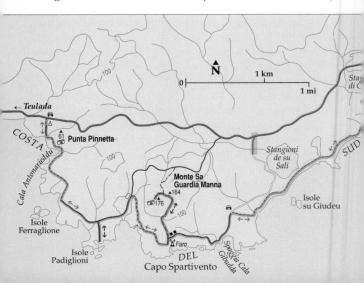

on Sardinia. Crowned by an old watchtower, Capo Malfatano is seen in the foreground, backed by Capo Teulada.

The path threads through low *macchia* and eventually
swings right before descending to a sandy cove; off the coast
are the Isole Ferraglione where seabirds nest (**35min**).
Follow the jeep track that begins at the cove, keeping left at
the fork reached in five minutes. (But first you could make
a short detour to the right; it would take you to the granite
coastline with the offshore Isole Padiglioni.)

Badly eroded in places, the track approaches a small inlet
before it rises again. Turn right just opposite a fenced-in area
on the left and continue to walk on the slopes of **Monte sa
Guardia Manna**. The trail begins to descend towards
another small inlet with a dilapidated jetty. Turn left at a
junction and climb the old trail to the lighthouse *(faro)* at
Capo Spartivento (**1h05min**). The building is sadly falling
into disrepair.

Now you can make an optional detour up to **Monte sa
Guardia Manna** (allow an extra 1.5km/0.9mi; 45min
return). Built on a supporting wall and originally cobbled
with stones, the old trail climbs through high *macchia*.
Among the many different species, the splendid specimens
of tree spurge *(Euphorbia dendroides)* here are particularly
attractive. Keep left when you cross a small saddle, to reach
the summit which is crowned by a derelict lookout post from
World War II. There is a splendid panorama of the entire
Costa del Sud, with the wooded Sulcis Mountains rising
further inland.

The main walk omits this ascent and continues along the
gravel track between the lighthouse buildings, descending
to the sheltered **Spaggia Cala Gibudda**. The azure water

here is almost irresistible — but another
splendid sandy beach is yet to come. Follow
the main track over a small rise, then turn right
opposite the large car park, to reach the
beginning of the glorious sandy BEACH
(**1h30min**). Dropping away gently into the
azure water, this splendid coastline is
reminiscent of the South Seas.

Tramp through the sand, following the
coast, or take off your shoes and paddle. The
Isole su Giudeu ('Jew Islands'; the origins of
the name are not known) rise off the shore
here, and the Stangioni de su Sali comes into
view on the left. Continue along the beach
until it ends at a small PROMONTORY (**1h**

Cala Antonarieddu

50min), where surfers are frequently seen. Cross the promontory to another beach. Go over the sand to the far end, then continue on a path that threads through high coastal *macchia*. Climb down some rocks to the last sandy beach on this walk. The Stagno di Chia stretches away inland.

At the end of this beach you reach another promontory, crowned by the **Torre di Chia**. Climb the path through the bushes to this old WATCHTOWER (**2h20min**), from where you enjoy a commanding view of the Costa del Sud.

Return the same way to your starting point at **Punta Pinnetta** (**4h40min**).

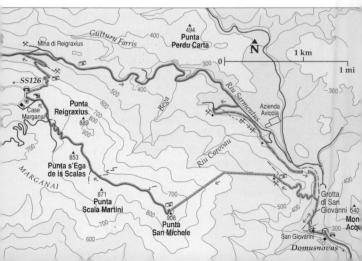

18 GROTTA DI SAN GIOVANNI • PUNTA SAN MICHELE • CASE MARGANAI • GUTTURU FARRIS • GROTTA DI SAN GIOVANNI

See map opposite

Distance/time: 14.1km/8.8mi; 5h 45min

Grade: strenuous, with climbs totalling 800m/2620ft; half the walk is pathless, along a steep and rocky fire-break. The rest follows good tracks and paths without any difficulties.

Equipment: see pages 53-54; walking sticks strongly recommended

How to get there and return: 🚗 by car from Iglesias (Car tour 4 at the

208km-point). Take the SS130 towards Cagliari, then turn off for Domusnovas. When you reach Domusnovas, follow signposting to the Grotta di San Giovanni through the village. The road passes abandoned mines and leads to the entrance of the cave and road tunnel; just before it you can park your car on either side of the road.

Photo: on the climb to Punta San Michele

Culminating at Punta San Michele (906m/2972ft), the southern flanks of the Iglesiente rise steeply from the Cixerri rift valley. The historic town of Iglesias ('Churches'), for which the mountain range was named, is spread out along these foothills. This was once the most important mining region on Sardinia and, indeed, in the whole of Italy. Lead, silver, copper and zinc mining began in the dim and distant past. Abandoned mines, large spoil heaps, and many galleries still testify to rich mineral deposits that were exploited over millennia; mining only came to a standstill a few decades ago.

Your starting point is the Grotta di San Giovanni, a 550m/yds-long limestone cavern. In the middle of the 19th century, a road was built through it in order to shorten the arduous route over the ridge. The walk begins with a steep and rocky climb to the Punta San Michele, from where there are splendid panoramic views. Then you follow a track to the forestry station of Marganai, before descending through a wooded valley. Your return is along an old railway track.

Start out at the CAR PARK in front of the entrance to the **Grotta di San Giovanni**. Cross the stream, leave the bar on your left, and climb the wide cobbled track to the CHAPEL OF **San Giovanni**; it stands in the middle of a beautiful olive grove (**3min**). Behind the chapel, follow the trail straight ahead uphill through the olive trees for about 75m/yds, then bear right at a fork (there is a red arrow on an olive tree and a wooden sign: CASE MARGANAI/MINIERA REIGRAXIUS/MALA CALZETTA). Straight away you pass a small metal shelter on the right and climb through the trees. RED-AND-WHITE FLASHES on rocks and trees confirm that you are on the right route.

116 Landscapes of Sardinia

Keep left on the main trail when you reach a fork. After a short while you meet a wider trail: turn right uphill. Soon ignore a sharp turn on your right. Bear right at the next fork that follows a short time later. At another fork, keep left on the main trail. Soon turn left uphill (the way straight ahead is signposted to 'Min Reigraxius') and reach a fork at once (**25min**): continue diagonally to the right (almost straight ahead); the fork to the right is where you will come back towards the end of the walk. The path gradually climbs in zigzags through scrub. Every once in a while you glimpse the crumbling stone wall that supports this old trail. As you ascend there are beautiful views down over the wooded saddle under which the Grotta di San Giovanni lies hidden.

You reach a RUINED BUILDING at the beginning of a rocky FIRE-BREAK overgrown with low scrub; to the left of it a gallery opens on the hillside (**1h10min**). There is an open view down into the valley, where you can see the abandoned Azienda Avicola (an old farm). The waymarked route bends to the right at the ruined building and crosses a fence straight away, to descend into the trees. Leave the trail here and climb up the hill alongside the fence — now without any waymarks. It is best to keep on the right-hand side of the fence. *Beware* of some deep holes in the ground at the outset. Huffing and puffing, you steeply climb along the fire-break.

Suddenly, the transmitter on top of Punta San Michele is seen above you. At this point the fire-break bends to the left (**1h40min**) and begins to climb straight to the summit. This section is even steeper and more rocky; on the last bit you have to scramble up on all fours. The splendid panorama from the top of **Punta San Michele** (**2h40min**) is ample compensation for the arduous climb. The fertile Cixerri rift valley is spread out far below you to the south; it separates the Iglesiente from the Sulcis, the mountain range rising on the opposite side. The town of Iglesias is seen in the southwest, surrounded by extensive mining areas. The view to the north encompasses the Iglesiente, an isolated mountain range partly covered with trees.

Follow the gravel track from the summit; it gradually winds downhill. After half an hour, ignore two left turns that follow almost immediately one after the other (**3h10min**). When you reach the **Case Marganai** (**3h25min**), there is a fenced-in HELIPAD on the right, while the FORESTRY STATION with its small botanical garden is on the left. This is a good place for a break. You can go through the garden, look at the plants and fill up your water bottle at the fountain. There is also a small bar with some benches just above the garden, where you can get refreshments.

Pass to the right of the botanical garden und reach a junction near a car park in an open space. (To the left, a tree-lined gravel road leads to the forestry house; the access road is straight ahead.) Leave the road here and turn right, following a grassy path through the meadow to the edge of the nearby woodland, where there is a wooden sign inscribed 'MIN. REIGRAXIUS/SENTIERO CAI'. Go through the wooden gate next to it and continue straight ahead on the faint but clear woodland trail; a WATER PIPE runs parallel with it on the left. The ground to the right is very rough and rocky because of the eroded limestone.

The trail rises slightly through the trees. Soon you reach a small rise where a view opens up towards the Iglesiente Mountains. Supported by a drystone wall, the old trail now zigzags beautifully down through the wood. Follow the main trail round a left bend, ignoring a minor trail that runs straight ahead past some overgrown ruins. Just beyond a GREEN IRON BARRIER, when you join a gravel track (**3h50min**), turn right downhill.

Straight away, ignore a minor track forking diagonally to the left behind an iron barrier. Some eight minutes later another track joins sharply from the left: continue straight ahead downhill. Affording fine views, the track runs through the wooded valley of the **Gutturu Farris**. Eventually you go through a barrier (open during the day; **4h40min**) and continue straight ahead (slightly to the right) on the main track. After about eight minutes you turn right on a side track that leads through a metal BARRIER PAINTED IN RED AND WHITE.

Climb this woodland track but, on the second bend to the right, turn off left on a minor track (**5h**). Following an old RAILWAY TRACK, this route contours along the wooded hillside. Soon you pass a RUINED BUILDING by a gallery. A short time later you cross a minor path; continue straight ahead. Pass another gallery and then another RUINED BUILDING. Keep right immediately beyond it — *don't* take the invitingly-wide track down to the left. Continue on the railway track past a RUINED HOUSE, then go through a SHORT TUNNEL (**5h25min**).

Continue straight ahead when you leave the tunnel. After less than ten minutes you regain the fork near the beginning of the walk. Now retrace your steps to the **Grotta di San Giovanni** (**5h45min**). The bar (open on weekends only) is most welcome for refreshments.

19 TORRENTE LENI • RIU D'ORIDDA • GUTTURU IS ABIS • RIU D'ORIDDA • PUNTA PISCINA IRGAS • RIU CANNISONI • TORRENTE LENI

Distance/time: 10.8km/6.7mi; 4h10min

Grade: moderate, with ascents totalling 415m/1360ft. For the most part, the walk follows clear tracks and paths which are partly waymarked with red paint and cairns.

Equipment: see pages 53-54

How to get there and return: 🚗 by car from Iglesias (Car tour 4 at the 208km-point). Take the SS130 towards Cagliari until you reach the sign-posted exit for Vallermosa after 24km. Follow the SS293 north via Vallermosa. Turn left to Villacidro when you meet the SS196 crossroads. After 4.5km, take the signposted exit to Villacidro. On entering this village, take the wide left turn (several signposts, including MONTI MANNU, DIGA, S SISINNIO, SAN GIUSEPPE). Now watch your cumulative km reading (set to 0 here). After 1.9km take the signposted right turn to the reservoir (DIGA SUL RIU LENI). The road passes a right turn to Villacidro after 400m and approaches the dam wall which is covered with greenery. Keep left at the fork by the dam wall, ignoring the 'Officio Diga' to the right. The road winds on the hillside above the reservoir. Turn left at the T-junction beyond a bridge (4.5km) that crosses an arm of the reservoir. After crossing the bridge over the main river (Torrente Leni) that feeds the reservoir (10.2km), you meet a T-junction: turn right on the gravel road. After 14.8km a fenced-in terraced nursery with the forestry house (Caserma Forestale) comes up on the right. Park your car below it, on the left-hand side of the gravel road.

Extending to the west of the eponymous reservoir, the Foresta Demaniale Montimannu comprises wild and rugged mountains, their rock — mainly granite and slate — dating from the Palaeozoic era. Springs flow for eight to nine months a year in this region; they feed two beautiful rivers which flow into the Torrente Leni below the Cantina Ferraris. The Riu d'Oridda is the most spectacular — a river cut deeply into the granite of the Concas de Piscina Irgas, where it has created beautiful rock pools and cascades. The woods are rich in different species; in addition to the native oaks, there are pines, chestnuts, cedars, cypresses, eucalypti

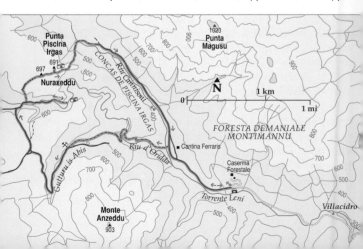

and mimosas. This circuit leads you through this magnificent landscape, affording splendid views throughout.

Before you set out, you can fill your water bottles at the spring next to the entrance gate to the nursery. **Start out** by following the gravel track straight ahead through the valley of the **Torrente Leni**; eucalyptus has been planted in the valley floor. Keep left at a fork and stay in the valley floor (the right-hand fork leads up to the Cantina Ferraris, a shepherds' outpost). Turn left by an olive tree in the open, park-like valley floor (the shepherds' outpost is seen up to your right from here) and cross the rushing river — either on the unstable-looking FOOTBRIDGE OR ON ROCKS (**20min**).

On the far side of the river the path snakes through *macchia*. Soon you pass a huge cork oak that bends over the **Riu d'Oridda**; mosses and ferns are growing on its gnarled branches. The trail rises through the trees above the river bed, before descending back down to it. When you regain the river, watch out for a LARGE ROCK ON THE BANK WITH IRON BARS sticking out of it (**35min**). Here you have to look out for the best spot to cross the river. Turn left on the far side and follow the path some 50m/yds along the river bank, before climbing an old, stony trail to the right (RED AND WHITE FAINT FLASH on a rock). This trail runs for some time above a stream bed which is glimpsed down to the right and gradually narrows to a path.

The path continues to rise and crosses to the right of the dry stream bed. Then it runs uphill in a sunny valley and crosses back to the left. You pass a huge fig tree, followed straight away by the drystone wall of an old CHARCOAL BURNING TERRACE on the left. Soon a spoil heap is seen on the right, followed by the ENTRANCE TO A GALLERY. Now the track widens and joins another track coming from behind you to the left (**1h10min**). Continue ahead through the **Gutturu is Abis** ('Ravine of the Bees'). As you gradually gain height, a beautiful view unfolds of the reddish cliffs opposite, culminating at Punta Magusu (1023m/3355ft). Eventually you cross a flat saddle and descend into a hollow where you bear right at the fork (**1h45min**).

Initially the track contours, before it begins to lead downhill. You reach the open river flats of the **Riu d'Oridda** which are densely covered with asphodelus and rock roses *(Cistus monspeliensis)* — a sea of white flowers in spring. Here the track branches (**1h55min**): turn right on the minor track and walk downstream. Soon the track crosses to the left side of the river. After some 75m/yds along the left bank, a faint, overgrown path rises to the left through the *macchia*. This is *easily missed;* it will be your route later in the walk. Ignore it for the moment and continue straight ahead downstream for a short detour to the beginning of the Oridda ravine.

Keep walking along the bank until the faint track you are on crosses back to the right-hand side of the river. If you look back now to the opposite (left) side of the river, you can see a spoil heap. The faint track crosses the river once more, leading you back to its left bank. Now continue on paths through a small coppice with some camp fires, until you are back at the RIVER BED (**2h10min**). Here the river leaves the flat valley bottom and the rocky RAVINE begins. The river is cut deeply into a granite massif. It would be far too dangerous to follow the course of the river through the ravine, since it flows through rock pools and over cascades — so savour the view and take a first break.

Then retrace your steps to the start of the faint overgrown path; it now comes up on your right (**2h20min**) and rises through *macchia,* to the left of a pine grove. This path is partly stony underfoot. Soon it curves to the left and climbs the hillside before petering out. Now head pathless up the steep hillside in a northeasterly direction towards some rocky outcrops. When you reach a WIRE-MESH FENCE continue uphill to the left of it. Eventually the distinct rocky peak of Nuraxeddu appears ahead of you; the wire fence leads across its highest point. Turn right through a gap in the fence at the foot of Nuraxeddu (**2h45min**). Now leave Nuraxeddu on your left and, pathless, walk straight ahead (east-northeast) through the *macchia* towards the highest summit (Punta Magusu) rising ahead of you. Faded red and white flashes and cairns will be of help but, if you keep heading towards the summit, you won't get lost.

After five minutes you reach the foot of another rocky peak, Punta Piscina Irgas, which rises to the left. On your right you look down into the deeply-etched Oridda gorge, where you can see a high waterfall. Now you can climb up to the left for a detour to the top of **Punta Piscina Irgas**, from where there is a magnificent panorama (**2h55min**). Descend the same way to the lower slopes and continue to walk east-northeast towards the highest peak. Following faint paths straight ahead along the rocky ridge, once again CAIRNS AND FADED WAYMARKS keep you on the right route.

Just before a rocky spur you reach a FLAT EARTHEN AREA with a campfire and stone seats, where several paths branch off (**3h10min**). Descend the trail to the left and keep left on the main trail at the fork soon encountered; it zigzags quite steeply downhill, partly on steps. Down in the valley you

You'll frequently come upon shepherds' outposts on your walks on Sardinia, with shepherds and (occasionally) shepherdesses tending their flocks in time-honoured fashion. A cuile (top right) is a typical sheepfold with shepherds' huts. Right: in the valley floor below the Cantina Ferraris

reach the **Riu Cannisoni** ('Cane River'). Turn right downstream, then cross the river bed on a FOOTBRIDGE (**3h25min**).

Continue to walk downstream along the left bank, initially in the shade of the trees, then in full sun. The track gradually becomes wider and you pass a fenced-in WATERWORKS. Eventually you regain the open area below the Cantina Ferraris (**3h55min**) and follow your outward route back through the valley of the **Torrente Leni** to where you left your car (**4h10min**).

20 TEMPIO DI ANTAS • GROTTA SU MANNAU • VILLAGIO NURAGICO • TEMPIO DI ANTAS • CAVE ROMANE • RIU DELLO SPIRITO SANTO • TEMPIO DI ANTAS

Distance/time: 16.5km/10.2mi; 5h30min

Grade: strenuous, with a total ascent of 540m/1770ft; some sections are rather steep. A word of caution: do not attempt the pathless section on the hillside in foggy or windy weather.

Equipment: see pages 53-54

How to get there and return: 🚗 by car from Iglesias on the SS126 to the north until you reach the signposted right turn for the TEMPIO DI ANTAS after 14.5km. The asphalt road ends after 2.3km at a small car park in front of the fenced-in area with the temple (Car tour 4 at the 225km-point).

Short walks: The route is a figure-of-eight, so you can easily break it up into two sections.

1   Tempio di Antas — Grotta su Mannau — Tempio di Antas (6.6km/ 4.1mi; 2h40min; moderate to strenuous, with a relatively steep climb of 350m/1150ft). Follow the main walk from the start to the 2h40min-point, when you come back to the temple again.

2   Tempio di Antas — Riu dello Spirito Santo — Tempio di Antas (10km/ 6.2mi; 2h55min; moderate to strenuous, with a climb of 190m/620ft). Follow the main walk from the visitor centre (2h40min-point) to the end.

Opening hours
Tempio di Antas: daily 9am-6pm
Grotta su Mannau: tel/fax 0781-580189 for information

Hidden in the Iglesiente Mountains is the Punic/Roman temple of Antas. It was dedicated to the legendary Sardus Pater, the deity of the Sardinian people. From here you follow an undulating trail through *macchia* and over a ridge down into a valley, where you come upon the entrance to the Grotta su Mannau, a splendid dripstone cavern which is open to the public. From here you continue steeply uphill on an old Roman road, before reaching an idyllic picnic spot. A pleasant trail takes you back to the temple via the remains of a Nuragic village. The second loop of this figure-of-eight climbs past a Roman quarry up to an old mining area, where you come upon some strange phenomena. Then you ramble along a ridge and through a green valley back to the temple.

Start out at the CAR PARK in front of the fenced-in area of the **Tempio di Antas**. The temple is hidden from here; you will visit it later, during the walk. Go back along the access road, past an *agriturismo* on the right, then leave the road shortly after it curves to the right by climbing a track diagonally up to the right. Leave this track after about 150m/yds (before it rises left towards a farm on the hill), and continue on the track that runs in the dip. Stay on the left side of this small valley, ignoring another track that crosses to the right. The track climbs alongside a wire-mesh fence, and you pass a PIGGERY on the right. The fence soon bends away to the left: continue straight ahead on the main track, past a left turn. The track runs through an area called **Sa Struvina** ('macchia'). Ignore an old trail running parallel with your track a few metres to the right; it is your return route.

At a fork (**30min**), keep left on the main track. It leads down into a slight depression, rises, and runs under a power line before descending again. Turn right uphill when the track branches down in a gully, and ignore a faint fork to the left almost immediately. Huffing and puffing, you climb steeply through the trees on this stony track. At the highest point you cross the SADDLE between **Monte Medau Matzei** on the left and the **Punta su Mannau** on the right (**55min**). Straight away you walk under the power line again, ignoring minor tracks branching off on both sides.

Now the track begins to descend. Leave it at the lowest point, just before it starts to rise again and the village of Fluminimaggiore comes into view to the north: fork right down a narrow path across scree. This woodland path/ trail zigzags steadily downhill; keep following it past any forks. Eventually the trees begin to thin out. You come upon three wooden picnic tables in the shady woodland, waiting for weary walkers. Steadily descending, you eventually meet the road down in the valley, by a large house. Turn right and follow the road to the car park at the **Grotta su Mannau** (**1h20min**). There are shady picnic spots and a drinking fountain; you can get refreshments in the visitor centre.

Continue straight ahead on the track past an ELECTRICITY SUB-STATION; now the ascent begins. Turn right at the first fork (some 150m/yds from the car park). Almost immediately you pass a PYLON on the left; there is an old CHARCOAL BURNING TERRACE on your right. You are now following an old Roman road that once connected Fluminimaggiore with Antas. For a while, a stone wall runs parallel with your track, on your right. Soon you reach a fork: keep right. Keep right again at the next fork soon afterwards. When you reach another fork, turn right for a few paces, then continue to climb straight uphill, ignoring the minor trail off to the right. The ascent gets even steeper now. An old mossy stone wall runs parallel with your trail, on the left, and more CHARCOAL BURNING TERRACES are seen along the route.

The old trail goes through a gap in the stone wall and now ascends to the left of it. Eventually the old stone wall turns off to the right, while you continue to climb on a path through scrub. Soon ignore a path branching off to the right and continue straight ahead on the old sunken trail that has

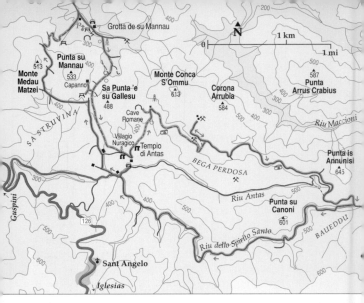

been cut into the rock. In times gone by Roman carts would rumble along here through the mountains; grooves are still evident in places. The sunken trail reaches a SADDLE (**2h 10min**) between the **Punta 'e su Gallesu** on the left and the **Punta su Mannau** on the right. Paths branch off on both sides. Ignore the path to the left, but follow the path to the right for a short detour. This path quickly leads to a fork. If you turn left, you'll come to a picnic table under a shady holm oak; a right turn would take you to a WOODEN SHELTER *(capanno)* — a good place to rest on a rainy day (**2h15min**).

The walk continues on the old trail. For a while your outward track runs parallel with this trail. The track eventually bends away to the right, while you keep left on the trail. It swings down to the left, then heads right, into a small valley. After walking some 80m/yds along the valley, bear left uphill on a path and contour along the sunny hillside. Soon follow a wire fence briefly, then go through a gap and continue along the hillside towards an old pylon. Join a track and follow it past the PYLON which rises nearby. Almost immediately after crossing a small ridge, you come upon the low walls of circular buildings on your right, the remains of an old Nuragic village (**Villagio Nuragico; 2h30min**). Soon you go through a wooden gate into the fenced-in area. The ANTAS VISITOR CENTRE (get your ticket here) is on your right (**2h35min**).

Now begin the second half of the walk. *(Short walk 1 returns to the car park after visiting the temple, Short walk 2 starts here.)* From the visitor centre continue to the nearby **Tempio di Antas** (**2h40min**). Go through the wooden gate beyond the temple and follow a path alongside the wire-mesh fence towards the lowest of THREE PYLONS standing on the opposite hillside. You enter a small valley with pear trees and a water pipe. Cross the irrigated field and continue uphill towards the middle pylon. Go through a WOODEN GATE at the end of the cultivated valley and continue to climb. Straight away you pass a CHARCOAL BURNING TERRACE on the right. Soon leave the track for a short detour on a path to the left, which leads within a few minutes to the Roman quarry (**Cave Romane**; 3h).

When you have inspected the site where stone for the temple was quarried in antiquity, return to the track and continue to climb. Almost immediately the route bends to the right (past a ruined stone house). Keep to the contouring trail which is now somewhat overgrown with rock roses (*Cistus monspeliensis*) as is rises slowly but steadily. It is actually an old railway track once used for transporting ore from the mine. There are beautiful views on the right over the temple down in the valley. You pass an eroded strip of hillside where an old mine gallery opens out (**3h15min**).

Nor far beyond here the trail bends to the left. Soon it leads into woodland and curves to the right, passing a path forking off left. Meet a T-junction and turn left; you will later return to this point. Affording brilliant views of the landscape in the heart of the Iglesiente, this track contours on the hillside. Eventually it curves to the right before petering out by a spoil heap and a RUINED BUILDING (**3h40min**). *Take great care now and watch every single step: this next section is cross-country, and there is a huge hole in the ground.* Climb the rough hillside on your right where, suddenly, a huge hole opens up in the ground. Keep a safe distance away from its edge! Further up the slope there is a dilapidated stone building; to the left of it a short tunnel leads through the rock to another deep, frightening-looking hole — again, take extra case here! Just above the building, yet another hole opens up in the ground. These holes, impressive but eerie, are one of the results of karstification, the process of erosion in limestone areas (see panel page 32).

Return to the track and retrace your steps. Go past the right turn from where you came and continue ahead on the ridge track. Monte Linas can be seen in the distance to the east, a mountain completely bare of trees. Keep walking straight on along the ridge at the same height; you go through a WIRE GATE and pass a few minor turn-offs. To the right a view opens up into the valley of the Riu Antas, where a shepherds' outpost can be seen. A large spoil heap down

TEMPIO DI ANTAS

Hidden in the hills of the Iglesiente, visitors come upon a reasonably-preserved temple from the time of the Roman emperors. Its fragmentary inscription carries the name Sardus Pater — god of the Sardinians. Excavations under the ruins of the broad front staircase revealed a previous Punic building. This temple was built at the end of the 6th century BC around a holy rock and extended at the beginning of the 3rd century BC. Inscriptions on votive articles show that the Punic temple had been dedicated to Sid, god of the hunt. Superficially, the Tempio di Antas looks like a perfectly classical building, but on closer view it becomes apparent that the spiritual influence behind the Roman temple remains Punic. This is also evident in the architecture: like its predecessor, the Roman building does not face east but northwest, and the inner sanctum is divided into two rooms with separate entrances (as in Punic temples), which can only be reached through purifying pits which were once filled with water. Roman borrowing of Punic religious belief is further evidenced in the use of the image of Sardus Pater, who is depicted on coins like the image of a Punic god, with a feather crown. Even the inscription on the Roman

temple indicates the fusion of Punic and Roman deities, as the temple has been dedicated to Sardus Pater BAB — BAB being another name for Sid.

Tempio di Antas (left); Nuragic statuettes of an archer with bow (top) and a chieftain with shepherd's crook

on the hillside is another testament to mining in the past.

Eventually you go through a WIRE GATE and join the track that climbs through the valley (**4h20min**). Turn left and follow the track for ten minutes, before forking sharp right on another track (signpost: BAUEDDU) that passes a farm on the right almost immediately and descends gradually through the valley of the **Riu dello Spirito Santo**. Ignoring any turn-offs, continue straight ahead for well over an hour, until you meet the asphalt road. Turn right for 200m/yds, back to the CAR PARK near the **Tempio di Antas** (**5h30min**).

21 UCC' AIDU • MONTE RASU • SA MELABRINA • SA UCCA 'E PADRONU • FATTORIA GIANNASI • CASA PISANELLA • CASERMA FORESTALE • UCC' AIDU

Distance/time: 16.7km/10.4mi; 5h35min

Grade: moderate-strenuous, with a total height gain of 600m/1970ft. The walk follows good tracks throughout, but it is rather long.

Equipment: see pages 53-54

How to get there and return: 🚌 only by car. From the central road junction in Bono, opposite the town hall, take the road rising diagonally; it climbs in hairpin bends above the village. Shortly after passing two rectangular parabolic antennas above the road on the right, you reach the pass of Ucc' Aidu (7.5km from the centre of Bono; Car tour 6 at the 158km-point). A stone wall flanks the right-hand side of the road; on the left a forestry track branches off towards Monte Rasu (recognised by its transmitter on top). Park beside the road.

Shorter walk: Omit the detours to Monte Rasu and to the former monastery (14.3km/8.9mi; 4h35min; moderate, with an overall climb of 450m/1480ft). Follow the main walk, but keep left when the track forks at the 30min-point; later, turn right when you reach the track junction of Sa Ucca 'e Padronu (at the 1h50min-point).

Enjoying solitude and stillness all along, this pleasant walk follows shady forestry tracks through dense oak woods and park-like pastureland with ancient, gnarled downy oaks. From Monte Rasu (1258m/4126ft), the highest summit in the Catena del Goceano, there is a splendid panoramic view over the mountain range and, indeed, most of northern Sardinia. A short detour takes you to the former Convento Francescano di Monte Rasu, the first Franciscan monastery to be founded on the island.

Start out at the pass of **Ucc' Aidu**: follow the track up to the left. Ignore a sharp turn on your left and another turn on the right (brown signpost: 'SEDDARDESILO'; picnic site). Keep on the main track when it bends left uphill, ignoring another track straight ahead. You are surrounded by low woodland with downy oaks and occasional hollies. It's often foggy up here in winter, so it's not surprising that lichen drips from the trees and ivy creeps up the trunks.

Eventually the track forks (**30min**). Here you can make a rewarding detour to the right, good visibility provided. *(But keep left for the Shorter walk.)* The climb takes you all the way to the transmitter on top of **Monte Rasu** ('Bare Mountain'; **50min**). There is a sweeping view over the light oak woods on the plateau that slopes slightly to the northwest; in the background you can see the table-topped mountains and volcanic cones of the Meilogu/Logudoro. To the east, beyond the Tirso Valley, the mountains of the Nuorese and the Barbagia extend as far as the eye can see.

Return to the fork in the track and turn right to continue. Almost immediately, bear right at another fork. Soon a fire-break affords a splendid view of the Tirso Valley. The village of Bono is seen far below, with Bottida a little bit further away. The ruined Castello di Burgos rises picturesquely on a granite spur. Bear left when the track forks on the flat saddle of **Sa Melabrina** ('Apple of the Hoar Frost', a name testifying to the harsh climate; **1h20min**) and pass a green iron gate straight away. Soon go through a WOODEN GATE and walk through the trees.

Keep right at the next fork. The track leaves the trees and descends gradually along the crest of the ridge. To the west you can see the wooded pastureland of the Catena del Goceano with the stud farm of Foresta di Burgos. After well over 15 minutes you go through another WOODEN GATE in a stone wall and reach the track junction on the saddle of **Sa Ucca 'e Padronu** ('Lord of the Manor's Pass'; **1h50min**). The walk will later continue to the right, but turn left now through the GREEN IRON GATE for a detour.

The concrete track descends between stone walls. Soon you reach the **Fattoria Giannasi** (**2h**). This manor dates from 1233, when the first Franciscan monastery on Sardinia was founded here; it existed until 1769. Today the statue of St Francis is kept in the church of San Raimondo in Bono. If anyone is near the house they will gladly let you into the small church, but the old monastic complex is not accessible.

Return to the saddle of **Sa Ucca 'e Padronu** (**2h20min**) and bear right down the track. Go past a sharp turn on your left and walk through an IRON GATE almost immediately. Keep left downhill at the following fork. Soon you reach a big junction in front of a WATER PUMPING HOUSE; five tracks join here (**2h35min**). Continue straight ahead on the second track from the left, passing to the right of the water pumping house.

The track gently descends through the oak wood. Eventually you walk through an IRON GATE and meet the road from Ucc' Aidu to Foresta di Burgos (**3h**). Turn left for a short distance, but leave the road just opposite the turn-off for Burgos, by turning right through the WOODEN GATE. Follow the field track to the left towards the enclosed farm, **Casa Pisanella**. The track swings to the right and leads to the front entrance to the farmyard (**3h10min**). Turn sharp right at the lowest point, on a grassy trail that initially contours along the hillside (do not confuse this with a minor trail that runs further downhill).

The trail gradually begins to descend through park-like open pastureland — an area called **Pedras Rujas** ('Red Stones'), with ancient downy oaks. The old cobbles of this beautiful trail are occasionally seen underfoot. Cross a small bridge over the **Riu Caramaurpes (3h15min)**. Soon you come upon a huge cork oak on the right with a hollow trunk; its gnarled branches soar into the sky. One wonders how much longer this giant tree will survive. Walk through an IRON GATE, cross the asphalt road and go through a gate just opposite, to continue on a forestry track. Keep going downhill past a right turn. The track leads into a gully where it crosses a stream before it rises again on the other side.

When a track joins from the left, continue uphill to the right. Ignore a left turn and keep climbing through an avenue of cedars, soon passing the buildings and workshops of the **Caserma Forestale** (forestry station). Leave the road here on a bend to the right and continue straight ahead on a track, to the old rose-coloured forestry house. Next to it, the picnic area of **Sa Puntighedda**, with tables and benches, is spread beneath the trees. To the right of the house, by the road, there's a fountain with good drinking water (**4h10min**).

Join the road and follow it a short way to the left, but

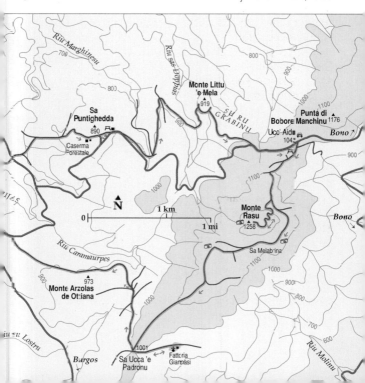

leave it at the end of the bend to the right and descend a forestry track, going through a GREEN IRON GATE immediately. The forestry track contours along the hillside. Ignore a left turn down into the valley of the Riu Marghinesu. Cross a track on the ridge, then immediately swing right into another valley.

Cross the **Riu sas Doppias** (**4h40min**) at the head of the valley and climb the slopes of **Monte Littu 'e Mela**. Follow the main track round a bend to the right, ignoring a minor trail straight ahead. When another track joins sharply from the left, continue straight ahead uphill on the ridge of **Su Ru Crabinu**.

After a steady climb you reach the asphalt road: turn left back to the pass of **Ucc' Aidu** (**5h35min**).

Wooded pastureland of the Catena del Goceano

Distance/time: 7.3km/4.5mi; 2h

Grade: easy, mostly level walking along the coastal path and track.

Equipment: see pages 53-54

How to get there and return: 🚗 only by car (13km) west of Alghero. Take the SS127 straight ahead past Fertilia and the Nuraghe Palmavera. Turn left when you meet a T-junction, following signposting for PORTO CONTE. The road ends at a car park at the Torre Nuova (Hotel Porto Conte). Savour the fine view of the bay, then drive back 500m to the Cantoniera Porto Conte, house N° 66, on the right, where there is good parking.

West of Alghero, a deep bay stretches inland which is almost totally enclosed. Its mouth is flanked by two precipitous promontories, the limestone cliffs of the Capo Caccia and the Punta del Giglio. This is Sardinia's best

Cliffs at the Punta del Giglio

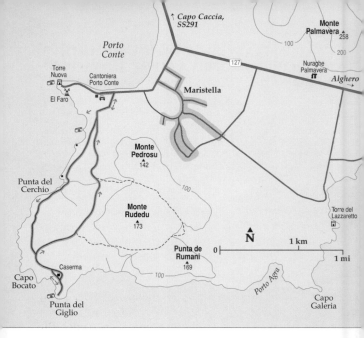

natural harbour. It is known as Porto Conte today, but in antiquity it had the more impressive name Portus Nympharum ('Port of the Nymphs'). Next to the lighthouse (El Faro), the old Torre Nuova rises on the tip of a small spit of land that juts into Porto Conte. Built to defend the port against corsair attacks, this imposing Spanish watchtower (like many others on Sardinia) dates back to the 17th century. From here there is a sweeping view of the magnificent bay. This smooth expanse of water almost looks like a lake, and its deep blue contrasts splendidly with the green sweep of pines surrounding the bay. Peaceful though it looks today, the tower reminds you of troubled times when the coastal inhabitants of the island lived under the constant threat of pirates. Numerous watchtowers were built along the coastlines to help protect the people.

This pleasant walk leads through pines and coastal *macchia* to the cliffs at Punta del Giglio, from where you enjoy a magnificent view of the opposite limestone cliffs of Capo Caccia. A special botanical feature of the area around Porto Conte is the dwarf fan palm *(Chamaerops humilis)* which flourishes in luxuriant abundance but is rarely encountered elsewhere on the island.

Start out at the **Cantoniera Porto Conte**. Follow the road for 150m/yds towards Alghero, then turn right up a track into the pines. After five minutes, just after a bend to the left, you reach a wide fork with red paint waymarking on a rock to the left. Bear right downhill here. Descend through woodland to the coast (**30min**). There is a splendid view of the promontory on the far side of the bay, plunging precipitously into the sea at Capo Caccia.

Soon you leave the coast as the track begins to climb; it is now very stony underfoot. Bear right at a junction on the scrubby limestone plateau. You can now see Punta del Giglio ahead of you to the right. Take either branch at the next fork; both tracks rejoin at an old World War II BARRACKS. Note the soldiers' *grafitti* inside the building, a grim testimony to times gone by. Among the inscriptions are *vinceremo* ('we will win'); *credere — obbedire — combatere* ('to believe — to obey — to fight'); *Quando torna il canona e veramente la voce della padria che chiava* ('When the big gun booms it's really the voice of the fatherland calling').

The screams of seagulls herald the nearby coast. The track peters out at the precipitously-plunging cliffs of **Punta del Giglio** ('Lily Point'; **1h**). Don't go too close to the edge of the cliff, as there is a sheer drop of more than 70m/230ft! Hidden in the *macchia* are dilapidated stone buildings and a gun emplacement dating back to World War II. To the west there is a splendid view of Capo Caccia ('Hunting Cape'), framing the western side of Porto Conte against the open sea. It was named after the practice of hunting wild boar in days gone by; the game could be easily driven into a corner on this narrow promontory.

Retrace your steps from Punta del Giglio as far as the junction where you originally climbed from the left. Keep right here on the main track and follow it along the plateau through park-like woodland with pines, cypresses and dwarf fan palms. Keep straight ahead on the main track, ignoring any turn-offs, until you meet the asphalt road again. Turn left to regain your car at the **Cantoniera Porto Conte** (**2h**).

Web sites focusing on Sardinia

You will find Sardinia in cyberspace, as well as in the Mediterranean! Here are a few major sites on the web focusing on Sardinia:

www.stieglitz.info is my homepage, with up-to-date information on Sardinia and other destinations, including many links

www.regione.sardegna.it is the island's official web site (with English version)

http://isolasarda.com is a privately run site in many languages (including English), with good links

http://web.tiscalinet.it/alterstampe/index.htm features ancient maps of Sardinia

Glossary (Sardinian and Italian)

abba — water
arcu — pass, saddle
atta — ridge
badde — valley
bacu — ravine, defile
badu — ford
bentu — wind
bivio — road junction
bosco — wood
bruncu — rounded hilltop
cala — bay
campo —field
capra — goat
campu — plain
casa — house
casa cantoniera — road keepers' building
cava — quarry, gorge
chiesa — church
coddu — hill, mound
codula — ravine, gorge

conca — peak, hollow
costa — flank, hillside
cuccuru — peak, hill
cuile — sheepfold
fonte — spring
foresta — forest
funtana, fontana — fountain
genna — pass, saddle
grotta — cave
gutturu — gorge
lago — lake
mesa — small plain
mitza — spring
monte — mountain
ovile — sheepfold
paule — marsh
pedra — stone
pineta — pine forest
ponte — bridge
pranu — plain, plateau
rifugio — refuge, hut

riu, rio — river
roccia — rock
saltu — uncultivated land, pastureland
scala — steep path
sentiero — path, trail
sorgente — spring
spiaggia — beach
strada bianca — gravel road
taccu — limestone buttress, pinnacle of rock
tanca — enclosed plot of land
tonneri — limestone plateau
torre — tower
torrente — torrent
ucca — cave, pass
valle — valley

● Index

This index contains geographical names only. For all other entries, see Contents, page 3. A page number in *italic type* refers to a map; **bold type** refers to a photograph. Both may be in addition to a text reference on the same page. **IT**: site; **✝** church or chapel.